Contemporary Chinese: An Introductory Text for Heritage Learners

当代华裔汉语

Contents

Preface...iii

Acknowledgements...iv

Introduction..v

    I.   The Chinese Language...v

    II.   The Chinese Sound system...v

    III. The Chinese Writing System...ix

    IV. Abbreviation of Grammatical Terms..xiv

Unit One   **Introducing Myself 自我介绍**..1

Lesson 1   Myself 我自己...2

Lesson 2   My Family 我的家...20

Unit Two   **My College Life 我的大学生活**...38

Lesson 3   My College 我的大学...39

Lesson 4   My Student Life 我的学生生活...56

Unit Three   **My Community 我的社区**...72

Lesson 5   My Neighborhood 我的街区...73

Lesson 6   Chinatown 中国城...89

Unit Four   **My Social Life 我的社交活动**..100

Lesson 7   Eating out in a Chinese Restaurant 在中餐馆吃饭.........................101

Lesson 8   Visiting a Friend's Family 在朋友家做客...................................117

Unit Five   **My Hobbies 我的爱好**..131

Lesson 9   Music 音乐 132

Lesson 10   Shopping 购物 146

Unit Six   Chinese Traditional Holidays 中国传统节日 160

Lesson 11   Chinese New Year 农历新年 161

Lesson 12   Mid-autumn Festival 中秋节 174

Unit Seven   Chinese Americans 美籍华人 186

Lesson 13   My Double Identity 我的双重身份 187

Lesson 14   Chinese in America 华人在美 198

Glossary Index 208

Preface

In recent years, more and more students of Chinese heritage are enrolling in Chinese language classes at American universities and colleges. Many of these students were either born in the United States or immigrated to this country when they were young children. At home, they may be exposed to spoken Chinese and even speak a dialect of the Chinese language to some extent, but they lack formal schooling in Mandarin Chinese, especially in reading and writing. Culturally, they identify themselves as Chinese Americans or "ABCs" (American-born Chinese) and tend to socialize with other Chinese Americans who share the same family backgrounds, interests, and values. They all feel the desire to learn more about their heritage language and culture in order to better communicate with their family members and other native speakers of Chinese, as well as to trace their Chinese roots. To serve the sociolinguistic needs of this Chinese student population, this textbook was compiled.

In keeping with the five goals (the 5 C's) of foreign language learning, <u>Contemporary Chinese: An Introductory Text for Heritage Learners</u> is especially designed for first-year American college students of Chinese descent who have some prior knowledge of the spoken language and its popular culture, but do not read or write Chinese by and large. Unlike most Chinese language textbooks for beginners, this communication-based course book is set in the cultural context of the United States rather than in China. The book takes students on a journey of self-discovery along with two fictional characters with whom they can closely identify with. The language is kept simple and authentic with common vocabulary and useful expressions reoccurring throughout the book. Best used with a learner-centered and interactive approach, this book is suitable for both classroom learning and self-study in one semester or one year.

This all-in-one textbook and workbook includes the following features:

- *Think and Share* piques students' interest by tapping into their prior knowledge of the topic under discussion;
- *Dialog* hones students' skills in pronunciation and character recognition by reading aloud conversations in contemporary spoken Chinese, following appropriate communicative and socio-cultural norms;
- *Answer Questions* elicits students' holistic understanding of the text by inferring information from the context;
- *Vocabulary* annotates all new vocabulary words in the text with *pinyin*, grammatical properties, and English translations;
- *Short Reading* provides a sample paragraph of written Chinese on the same subject matter as *Dialog*, reinforcing the vocabulary and sentence structure previously learned in a slightly more formal style;

- *Task* introduces all kinds of authentic communicative activities (interpretive, interactive, and presentational) in various setups (individual, pair, group, class), allowing students to apply what they have just learned to real-life situations;
- *Character Notes* introduces common radicals with examples to follow;
- *Grammar and Usage* provides succinct and jargon-free explanation of some grammar trouble spots that appear in the text, followed by illustrative examples;
- *Cultural Information* elaborates on the cultural points brought up in the text;
- *Pattern Drill* offers additional practice with unique and difficult sentence structure especially for non-Mandarin speakers while recycling learned vocabulary;
- *Pronunciation Drill* focuses on certain troublesome pronunciation in Mandarin Chinese in the form of rhymes and poems, with content more or less related to the topic of each chapter;
- *Exercises* offers more practice with the target language by means of character writing, word matching, character analysis, word and sentence formation, filling in the blanks, translation, error correction, paragraph writing, and small internet research projects outside of the classroom.

This book introduces approximately 600 Chinese characters and vocabulary words. By the end of this book, students will be able to conduct everyday conversations about some common topics in Mandarin Chinese, read and write short paragraphs (up to 100 Chinese characters) about these topics, and gain a better appreciation of Chinese culture and the history of Chinese people in America. It is hoped that by studying this book, students will take pride in their Chinese-American heritage and identity, laying a solid foundation for further study in the Chinese language.

Acknowledgements

This project started in 2010 under the encouragement of Eriko Sato, author of <u>Contemporary Japanese: An Introductory Textbook for College Students</u>, who inspired me to write a unique textbook that is user-friendly and fun for beginning learners of Chinese language. I am greatly indebted to Kamling Wong and Xiaoping Ha, my Chinese colleagues at Stony Brook University, for testing this textbook in their classes and giving me invaluable feedback and generous help with revising the textbook. I am also deeply grateful to all my student assistants, Tannong Zheng, Xiaowen Chen, Jiaqi Liu, Changda Li, Yongsang Yu, Benny Lam, and Frances Weinberg, and Lu Zeng, who were involved in various phases of the production. Last but not least, I would like to thank my family for their unconditional support. This book would not have been possible if not for all their assistance and support.

Dongmei Zeng, D. A.

Stony Brook University, Stony Brook, New York

2018

Introduction

I.   The Chinese Language

汉语 (hànyǔ, 'the Chinese language') is a family of dialects spoken by the Han people, the largest ethnic group in China. With about a quarter of the world's population as its native speakers, Chinese is the most spoken language in the world and the third most spoken language in the United States.

Following are some important facts about the Chinese language:

- It consists of seven main branches of dialects, which share the same writing system but can be mutually unintelligible when spoken. These include Mandarin (Northern China), Min (Fujian and Taiwan), Xiang (Hunan), Gan (Jiangxi), Wu (Jiangsu and Zhejiang), Hakka (Guandong and Guangxi), and Yue (Guangdong).

- It is a tonal language. The same syllable spoken with different tones can have different meanings. Mandarin has 4 tones plus an unstressed neutral tone.

- It has a large number of homophones, syllables that sound alike but have different meanings.

- It is originally monosyllabic in that each syllable corresponds to a word. However, modern Chinese relies heavily on compounding, which combines monosyllabic words to form polysyllabic words with new meanings.

- It is not an inflectional language. There are no word endings to indicate person, number, gender, case, tense or mood. The meaning of a sentence heavily depends on the context. Grammatical relationships are shown either by word order or by the use of independent grammatical particles such as 了 (le, perfective), 过 (guò, experiential), and 着 (zhe, progressive or stative).

- It is topic-prominent. Although the basic word order is subject-verb-object, the subject does not always appear at the beginning of a sentence. Instead, it is the topic, or whatever the sentence is about, that usually starts a sentence.

II.   The Chinese Sound System

Despite wide regional dialectal differences in the Chinese language, for centuries, the Chinese governments have established and been promoting a unified pronunciation based on the Beijing dialect for official communication. Today, this standard form of Mandarin, known as 普通话 (pǔtōnghuà, 'the Common Speech') in Mainland China, 国语 (guóyǔ, 'the National Language') in Taiwan, and 华语 (huáyǔ, 'the Chinese Language') in Singapore and other Chinese diaspora, is widely spoken in these parts of the world. In fact, it has become synonymous with 'Chinese language'. For convenience, we will use the terms 'Mandarin' and 'Chinese' interchangeably in this book.

Also in the past few centuries, many attempts have been made to transcribe the Chinese sound system with Latin alphabet to facilitate learning Chinese pronunciation and looking up Chinese characters in dictionaries. Today, the most widely adopted phonetic transcription is 拼音 (pīnyīn, 'spell sound'), developed in Mainland China in the 1950s. It employs 26 Roman letters plus four tonal marks to indicate the sound in Mandarin Chinese. Below is a brief introduction to the *pinyin* system.

There are over twelve hundred meaningful syllables in Mandarin Chinese. Each syllable is usually made up of three parts: an initial (consonant), a final (vowel or vowel + nasal) and a tone.

1. Initials
    There are 21 initials in Mandarin Chinese.

	Unaspirated	Aspirated	Nasal	Fricative	Voiced
Labial	b	p	m	f	
Alveolar	d	t	n		l
Velar	g	k		h	
Palatal	j	q		x	
Dental Sibilant	z	c		s	
Retroflex	zh	ch		sh	r

2. Finals
    There are 36 finals in Mandarin Chinese.

Simple finals	a	o	e	i		u	ü
Compound finals	ai ao	ou	ei er	ia iao ie iu(iou)		ua uai ui(uei) uo	üe(yüe)
Nasal finals	an ang	ong	en eng	in ing ian iang iong		uan un(uen) uang ueng	üan ün(üen)

Notes:

ü is written as u after /j/, /q/, /x/, /y/; hence, ju, qu, xu, yu, but the pronunciation does not change.

i is pronounced as ɨ after z, c, s, zh, ch, sh, r.

Pinyin Chart

	b	p	m	f	d	t	n	l	g	k	h	z	c	s	zh	ch	sh	r	j	q	x	⁂
a	ba	pa	ma	fa	da	ta	na	la	ga	ka	ha	za	ca	sa	zha	cha	sha					a
o	bo	po	mo	fo																		o
e			me		de	te	ne	le	ge	ke	he	ze	ce	se	zhe	che	she	re				e
ai	bai	pai	mai		dai	tai	nai	lai	gai	kai	hai	zai	cai	sai	zhai	chai	shai					ai
ei	bei	pei	mei	fei	dei	tei	nei	lei	gei	kei	hei	zei			zhei		shei					ei
ao	bao	pao	mao		dao	tao	nao	lao	gao	kao	hao	zao	cao	sao	zhao	chao	shao	rao				ao
ou		pou	mou	fou	dou	tou	nou	lou	gou	kou	hou	zou	cou	sou	zhou	chou	shou	rou				ou
an	ban	pan	man	fan	dan	tan	nan	lan	gan	kan	han	zan	can	san	zhan	chan	shan	ran				an
ang	bang	pang	mang	fang	dang	tang	nang	lang	gang	kang	hang	zang	cang	sang	zhang	chang	shang	rang				ang
en	ben	pen	men	fen	den		nen		gen	ken	hen	zen	cen	sen	zhen	chen	shen	ren				en
eng	beng	peng	meng	feng	deng	teng	neng	leng	geng	keng	heng	zeng	ceng	seng	zheng	cheng	sheng	reng				eng
ong					dong	tong	nong	long	gong	kong	hong	zong	cong	song	zhong	chong		rong				ong
u	bu	pu	mu	fu	du	tu	nu	lu	gu	ku	hu	zu	cu	su	zhu	chu	shu	ru				wu *
ua									gua	kua	hua				zhua	chua	shua	rua				wa *
uo					duo	tuo	nuo	luo	guo	kuo	huo	zuo	cuo	suo	zhuo	chuo	shuo	ruo				wo *
uai									guai	kuai	huai				zhuai	chuai	shuai					wai *
ui					dui	tui			gui	kui	hui	zui	cui	sui	zhui	chui	shui	rui				wei * 1
uan					duan	tuan	nuan	luan	guan	kuan	huan	zuan	cuan	suan	zhuan	chuan	shuan	ruan				wan *
uang									guang	kuang	huang				zhuang	chuang	shuang					wang *
un					dun	tun	nun	lun	gun	kun	hun	zun	cun	sun	zhun	chun	shun	run				wen * 2
ueng																						weng *
i	bi	pi	mi		di	ti	ni	li				zi †	ci †	si †	zhi ‡	chi ‡	shi ‡	ri ‡	ji	qi	xi	yi +
ia					dia			lia											jia	qia	xia	ya +
ie	bie	pie	mie		die	tie	nie	lie											jie	qie	xie	ye +
iao	biao	piao	miao		diao	tiao	niao	liao											jiao	qiao	xiao	yao +
iu			miu		diu		niu	liu											jiu	qiu	xiu	you + 3
ian	bian	pian	mian		dian	tian	nian	lian											jian	qian	xian	yan +
iang							niang	liang											jiang	qiang	xiang	yang +
in	bin	pin	min				nin	lin											jin	qin	xin	yin +
ing	bing	ping	ming		ding	ting	ning	ling											jing	qing	xing	ying +
iong																			jiong	qiong	xiong	yong +
ü							nü	lü											ju ※	qu ※	xu ※	yu ※
üe							nüe	lüe											jue ※	que ※	xue ※	yue ※
üan																			juan ※	quan ※	xuan ※	yuan ※
ün																			jun ※	qun ※	xun ※	yun ※

Source: Pinyin.info

3. Tones

There are four basic tones in Mandarin Chinese. A syllable with the same initial and final but different tones has different meanings. For example:

The first tone (high-level pitch)	bā	八	'eight'
The second tone (high rising)	bá	拔	'to pull'
The third tone (low falling-rising)	bǎ	把	'to hold'
The four tone (high-falling)	bà	爸	'dad'

In addition, some syllables in Mandarin Chinese are reduced in length and forcefulness in pronunciation. They are said to have a neutral tone, which is represented with no tonal mark in *pinyin*. For example:

māma	妈妈	'mom'
sheìde	谁的	'whose'
nǐne	你呢	'how about you'
bàba	爸爸	'dad'

Moreover, some syllables change tones depending on the phonological environment in which they occur. This phenomenon is called 'tone sandhi'. Below are some tone sandhi rules in Mandarin.

1) Third-tone Sandhi

When a third tone is followed by another third tone, the first third tone is pronounced as a second tone even though it is written as a third tone. For example:

nǐ → níhǎo	你好	'Hello'
hěn → hénhǎo	很好	'very well'

2) Tone Sandhi of '一'

'一' (yī, 'one') is pronounced as a first tone when alone. However, when it occurs before a first tone, second tone, or third tone, it is pronounced as a fourth tone. When it occurs before a fourth tone, it is pronounced as a second tone. For example:

yìxiē	一些	'some'
yìnián	一年	'one year'
yìqǐ	一起	'together'
yícì	一次	'one time'

3) Tone Sandhi of '不'

'不' (bù, 'no') is normally pronounced as a forth tone, but it is pronounced as a second tone when it occurs before a fourth tone. For example:

bùgāo	不高	'not tall'
bùbái	不白	'not white'
bùhǎo	不好	'not good'
búhuài	不坏	'not bad'

Pinyin Exercises

1. Read the following pairs of syllables in Chinese. Pay attention to the contrasts in the initials.

    1) zì   zhì   2) cī   chī   3) sì   shì   4) xī   sī

    5) nǔ   lǔ   6) zuò   cuò   7) suō   ruò   8) jú   qú   xú

2. Read the following pairs of syllables. Pay attention to the contrasts in the finals.

    1) duī   diū   2) liè   lèi   3) yòu   yào   4) nín   níng

    5) zǒu   zuǒ   6) dié   děi   7) qué   qún   8) cái   cán

3. Read the following words in *pinyin*. Pay attention to tone changes.

    1) 可口 kěkǒu   2) 祈祷 qídǎo   3) 美好 měihǎo   4) 腼腆 miǎntiǎn

    5) 不良 bùliáng   6) 不差 búchà   7) 一出 yìchū   8) 一样 yíyàng

III.   The Chinese Writing System

The Chinese script is the world's oldest writing system still in use today. It appeared as a fully developed writing system in the Shang Dynasty (14th to 11th centuries BC). Most of the writings of that time were found on oracle bones and tortoise shells in the form of short divinatory texts. Since that time, the Chinese script has gone through long periods of evolution before developing into the Chinese characters we know today.

Chinese characters are logographic in that each symbol represents a meaningful syllable in Chinese. Although a small number of Chinese characters are pictographs, picture-like writings that resemble the objects they represent, such as 目 (mù, 'eye'), 水 (shuǐ, 'water'), 山 (shān, 'mountain'), most Chinese characters are semantic-phonetic compounds in that each character is composed of a graph that suggests its basic meaning and another graph that hints at its sound. For example, the character 妈 (mā, 'mother') consists of a semantic element 女 (nǔ, 'female') and a phonetic element 马 (mǎ, 'horse'). The semantic element is also called a *radical*, which classifies characters according to their shared semantic properties. For example, 妈 (mā, 'mother'), 姨 (yí, 'aunt'), 姑 (gū, 'aunt'), 姐 (jiě, 'older sister'), 妹 (mèi, 'younger sister) all share the same radical 女 (nǔ, 'female') and the property of being female. As a large number of Chinese characters are of the semantic-phonetic nature, one can sometimes guess the meaning and pronunciation of an unknown character by looking at its semantic and phonetic components respectively.

Currently, there are two versions of the Chinese script in use---traditional characters and simplified characters. The traditional character version has been in existence for about 2000 years, and it is still in use in Taiwan, Hong Kong, and many overseas Chinese communities. The simplified character version was adopted in Mainland China in the 1950s in an effort to promote literacy. It is widely used in Mainland China, Singapore, and overseas Chinese communities along with the traditional character version. There are over 2000 simplified characters in all.

Although the largest Chinese dictionary lists about 86,000 characters, the actual number of characters in ordinary use is around 3,500. An ordinary literate Chinese person knows and uses somewhere between 5,000 and 7,000 Chinese characters. Even with 3000 commonly-used characters, a proficient learner should be able to read a Chinese newspaper with the help of a dictionary.

All Chinese characters are composed of a number of strokes put together according to some basic principles. It is important for the learner to practice the basic strokes following the proper order. That way, one will be more likely to form well-balanced characters with the correct number of strokes going in the right direction.

Rules for stroke order:

1. From top to bottom.   Example: 主　上
2. From left to right.   Example: 们　的
3. Middle before side.   Example: 小　少
4. Horizontal before vertical strokes.   Example: 十　下
5. Left-falling before right-falling.   Example: 人　大
6. Boxes before strokes that cut through.   Example: 中　申
7. From outer strokes to inside ones, and the sealing stroke last.   Example: 同　国
8. Enclosed strokes before enclosing strokes on the left and bottom. Example: 这　远

Basic Strokes in Chinese Characters

1. The following are the first six strokes, the fundamental ones:

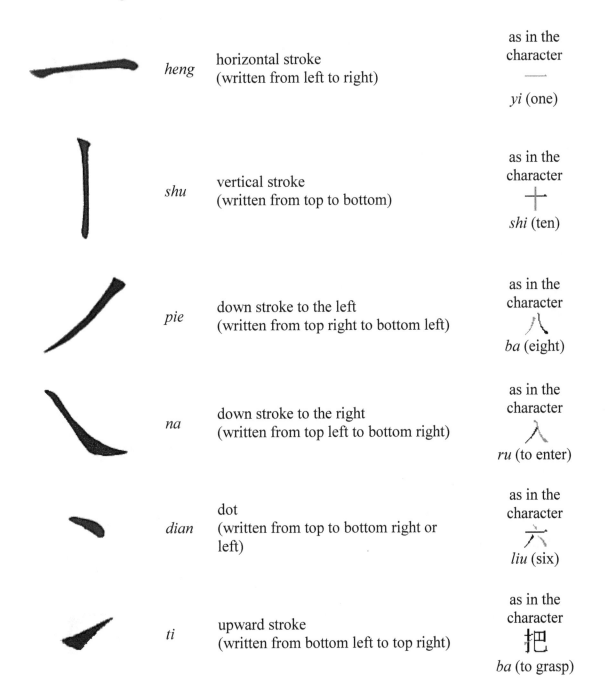

—	*heng*	horizontal stroke (written from left to right)	as in the character — *yi* (one)
|	*shu*	vertical stroke (written from top to bottom)	as in the character 十 *shi* (ten)
/	*pie*	down stroke to the left (written from top right to bottom left)	as in the character 八 *ba* (eight)
\	*na*	down stroke to the right (written from top left to bottom right)	as in the character 入 *ru* (to enter)
`	*dian*	dot (written from top to bottom right or left)	as in the character 六 *liu* (six)
/	*ti*	upward stroke (written from bottom left to top right)	as in the character 把 *ba* (to grasp)

2. The last two strokes have several different variations. The first group is composed by five strokes with a hook:

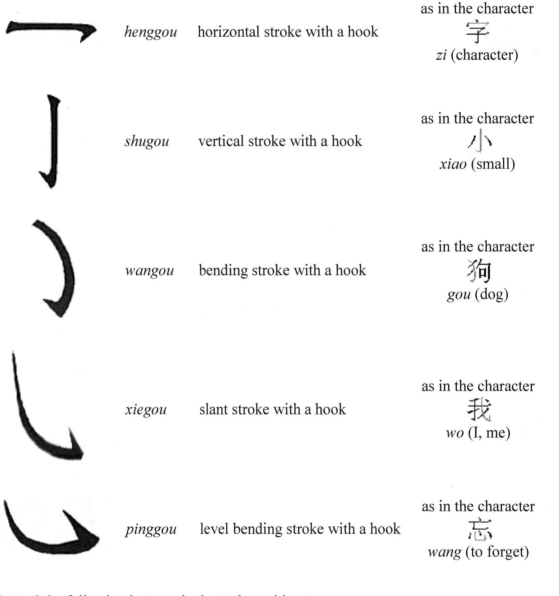

			as in the character
henggou	horizontal stroke with a hook		字 *zi* (character)
shugou	vertical stroke with a hook		小 *xiao* (small)
wangou	bending stroke with a hook		狗 *gou* (dog)
xiegou	slant stroke with a hook		我 *wo* (I, me)
pinggou	level bending stroke with a hook		忘 *wang* (to forget)

3. And the following by two single strokes with a turn:

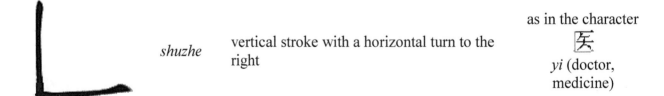

shuzhe vertical stroke with a horizontal turn to the right

as in the character
医
yi (doctor, medicine)

hengzhe　　horizontal stroke with a vertical turn

as in the character

口

kou (mouth)

4. Combined strokes are made out of basic ones. The following are a few examples:

shuwangou　　vertical stroke combined with a level bending stroke with a hook

as in the character

也

ye (also)

piedian　　down stroke to the left combined with a dot

as in the character

女

nu (woman)

shuzhezhegou　　vertical stroke with a double turn and a hook

as in the character

马

ma (horse)

Source: ClearChinese.com

IV.   Abbreviations of Grammatical Terms

Adj   adjectives

Adv   adverbs

Aux   auxiliary verbs

Co-v   co-verb

Conj   conjunctions

Idiom   idiomatic expression

Int   interjection

M   measure word

N   noun

Nu   numerals

Part   particles

Prep   prepositions

Pron   pronouns

V   verb

Unit One 第一单元

Introducing Myself 自我介绍

Lesson 1 第一课　Myself 我自己

Think and Share 想想说说

1. 你怎样用中文来做自我介绍？How do you introduce yourself in Chinese?
2. 中国人一般怎样介绍自己的名字？How do Chinese generally introduce their names?
3. 中国人可不可以问对方的年龄？Is it acceptable for Chinese to ask about each other's age?
4. 你第一次跟人见面打招呼的时候一般做什么动作？What body language do you normally use when you greet someone you meet for the first time?

Dialogue 对话

陈凯文：嗨，你好！

王丽莉：你好！

陈凯文：我叫陈凯文。你叫什么名字？

王丽莉：我姓王，叫丽莉。

陈凯文：我是大二学生，你呢？

王丽莉：我是大一学生。

陈凯文：你是属猴的，对吧？

王丽莉：对呀，我属猴。你是属羊的吗？

陈凯文：是的，我今年十九岁。

王丽莉：你是学什么专业的？

陈凯文：我学商。你呢？

王丽莉：我学医。

陈凯文：认识你很高兴。

王丽莉：我也很高兴认识你。

Answer Questions 回答问题

1. 陈凯文是属什么的？What is Kevin Chen's Chinese zodiac sign?
2. 他今年几岁？How old is he?
3. 王丽莉是属什么的？What is Lily Wang's Chinese zodiac sign?

4. 她今年几岁？How old is she?

Vocabulary 生词

1. 自我	zìwǒ	adj	self
2. 介绍	jièshào	v/n	to introduce; introduction
3. 我	wǒ	pron	I; me
4. 自己	zìjǐ	pron	self
5. 嗨	hài	int	hi
6. 你	nǐ	pron	you
7. 好	hǎo	adj	good
8. 你好	nǐhǎo	idiom	hello
9. 叫	jiào	v	to call; to be called by the name of
10. 什么	shénme	pron	what
11. 名字	míngzi	n	name (full name or given name)
12. 姓	xìng	v/n	to be surnamed; family name
13. 是	shì	v	to be
14. 大二	dàèr	n	(abbr) college sophomore year
15. 呢	ne	part	(to indicate reciprocal or rhetorical question)
16. 大一	dàyī	n	(abbr) college freshman year
17. 学生	xuésheng	n	student
18. 属	shǔ	v	to belong; to be born in the lunar year
19. 猴	hóu	n	monkey
20. 的	de	part	(to indicate possession, modification, or to soften speech)
21. 对	duì	adj	correct
22. 吧	ba	part	(to solicit agreement)
23. 呀	ya	part	(to soften forcefulness of speech)

3

24. 羊	yáng	n	ram
25. 吗	ma	part	(to form a yes/no question)
26. 今年	jīnnián	n	this year
27. 十九	shíjiǔ	nu	nineteen
28. 岁	suì	m	years of age
29. 学	xué	v/n	to study; to learn; study of
30. 专业	zhuānyè	n	major
31. 商	shāng	n	(abbr) business
32. 医	yī	n	(abbr) medical science
33. 认识	rènshi	v	to know; to get to know (someone)
34. 很	hěn	adv	very
35. 高兴	gāoxìng	adj	glad
36. 也	yě	adv	also

Proper Nouns 专有名词

1. 陈凯文	chén kǎiwén	Kevin Chen
2. 王丽莉	wáng lìli	Lily Wang

Short Reading 阅读短文

　　大家好！我来自我介绍一下。我叫陈凯文，今年十九岁，是大学二年级学生，主修商学，很高兴能认识大家。这是王丽莉，她是大学一年级学生，主修医学，她也很高兴能跟大家一起学中文。

Answer Questions 回答问题

1. 陈凯文是大学几年级学生？Which year of college is Kevin Chen in?
2. 他是学什么专业的？What is his major?
3. 王丽莉是大学几年级学生？Which year of college is Lily Wang in?
4. 她主修什么？What is her major?

Vocabulary 生词

1. 大家	dàjiā	n	everybody

4

2. 来	lái	v	to come; be about to
3. 一下	yíxià	adv	a little while
4. 大学	dàxué	n	college; university
5. 年级	niánjí	n	grade; year in school
6. 主修	zhǔxiū	v	to major in
7. 能	néng	aux	can; to be able to
8. 这	zhè	pron	this
9. 她	tā	pron	she; her
10. 跟	gēn	prep	with
11. 一起	yìqǐ	adv	together
12. 中文	zhōngwén	n	Chinese language

Supplementary Vocabulary 补充生词

1. 计算机学	jìsuànjīxué	n	computer science
2. 文学	wénxué	n	literature
3. 数学	shùxué	n	mathematics
4. 经济学	jīngjìxué	n	economics
5. 心理学	xīnlǐxué	n	psychology
6. 历史学	lìshǐxué	n	history
7. 物理学	wùlǐxué	n	physics
8. 化学	huàxué	n	chemistry
9. 工程	gōngchéng	n	engineering
10. 美术	měishù	n	art

Task 1 Pair Activity 双人活动

Find a partner in your class and ask about one other's name, year and major in college, Chinese zodiac sign and guess his/her age. Please be sure to use appropriate body language when introducing yourself.

Task 2 Group Activity 小组活动

Form groups of four and introduce your partner to your group. Please mention his/her name, Chinese zodiac sign, year and major in college.

Task 3 Class Activity 全班活动

Sit in a circle and pick someone to say his/her name first by saying 我叫... The next person in line will name the previous person by saying 你叫... before saying his/her own name 我叫... Repeat the process until the end of the line.

Character Notes 汉字讲解

As mentioned in the introduction, most Chinese characters are semantic-phonetic compounds in that each character is composed of a graph that suggests its basic meaning and another graph that hints at its sound. The semantic element is also called a *radical*, which classifies characters according to their shared semantic properties. The key to learning the Chinese character is to master the 214 commonly used radicals, which will give you the clue to the meaning of each character . Below is a list of characters in this chapter that share the most commonly used radicals:

1. 口字旁

The 'mouth radical' implies exclamation, question, or anything that inovloves the mouth. For example:

嗨	hài	int	hi
叫	jiào	v	to call; to be called by the name of
呢	ne	part	(to indicate reciprocal or rhetorical question)
吧	ba	part	(to solicit agreement)
呀	ya	part	(to soften forcefulness of speech)
吗	ma	part	(to form a yes/no question)
名	míng	n	name

2. 单人旁/人字头

The 'single person radical' implies that the character has something to do with a person. For example:

你	nǐ	pron	you
什	shén	pron	(part of the word 'what')
介	jiès	v/n	(part of the word 'introduce')
今	jīn	a	current; present (time)

3. 女字旁

The 'female radical' implies 'faminiety'. For example:

好	hǎo	adj	good
姓	xìng	v/n	to be surnamed; family name
她	tā	pron	she; her

4. 言字旁

The 'speech radical' implies 'the use of language'. For example:

认识	rènshi	v	to know; to get to know (someone)

Besides the radical, it is also important to learn the rest of the character is usually another character on its own, borrowed to indicate the approximate sound of the compound character. By breaking down an unknown character to its known semantic-phonetic components, you can quickly enlarge your Chinese vocabulary. For example, you may not know the character 哦 (Ó, oh), but by looking at its radical 口 and the rest of the character 我, you can guess it is probably an interjection that sounds like 我 (wǒ). Likewise, if you know the whole character but not its parts, you can also guess the meaning or sound of the parts by looking at the whole character. For example, you have learned the character 吗 in this chapter and the radical 口, you would probably be able to guess that the simple character 马 is pronounced like *ma*; given the phonetic and contextual clues, you may also be able to guess it means 'horse'.

Grammar and Usage 语法讲解

1. 你叫什么名字？ 'What's your name?' Unlike English, information question words in Chinese like 什么 'what' or 怎样 'how' do not typically appear at the beginning of a sentence. They remain in their places as in a statement. For example:
   1) 你几岁了？ How old are you?
   2) 你是学什么专业的？ What's your major?
   3) 你们是怎么认识的？ How did you get to know each other?

2. 呢，吧，呀，吗 are particles used at the end of a sentence to convey various mood of speech. 呢 is usually used to form a reciprocal or rhetorical question. 吧 is often used by the speaker to make a guess. 呀 conveys surprise, agreement,

defensiveness, urge, etc. 吗 is the most common question marker. For example:

1) 你是大二学生吧？You must be college sophomore, right?

2) 对呀，我是大二学生。That's right. I am college sophomore.

3) 你呢？How about you?

4) 你是属羊的吗？Were you born in the Year of the Ram?

3. 是的 means 'yes.' For example:

你是大一学生吗？Are you a freshman?

是的，我是大一学生。Yes, I am a freshman in college.

是...的 is also used around an verb phrase to emphasize certain facts such as 'what', 'when', 'why', 'where', 'how', etc. somewhat like the English sentence 'it is ...that...'

你是属猴的吧 emphasizes the fact 'born in the year of monkey.' For example:

1)   你是属羊的吧？You were *born in the Year of the Ram*, right?

2)   你是学什么专业的？*What* do you study for your major?

3)   你家是从哪里来的？*Where* is your family from?

4)   你们是怎么认识的？*How* did you get to know each other?

Please be sure not to confuse 是...的 'it is … that…' with the copula verb 是 'to be'. For example:

1)   你是中国人吗? Are you Chinese? *你是中国人的吗？

2)   我是大一学生。I am a college freshman. *我是大一学生的。

4.   认识你很高兴 and 很高兴认识你 both mean 'pleased to meet you.'
很 is often used before an adjective whether or not it means 'very'. For example, in the sentence here, 很高兴 simply means 'glad', not 'very glad'. In Chinese, unlike English, adjectives such as 高兴 can function as predicates; therefore, predicative adjectives do not need the copula verb 是 'to be.' For example:

1)   你好吗？How are you? *你是好吗？

2)   我很好。I am fine. *我是很好。

3)   你今年几岁？How old are you? *你今年是几岁？

5.   In Chinese discourse, as long as the topic remains the same, it is unnecessary to repeat the subject of each sentence as it is in English. For example, in the discourse 我叫陈凯文，今年十九岁，是大学二年级学生，主修商学，很高兴能认识大家，'My name is Kevin Chen. I am nineteen years old. I am college sophomore. I major in

business. I am pleased to meet you', it is best not to repeat 我 in the subsequent sentences. Also, a comma is used to separate sentences in a discourse rather than a period.

6. Chinese Numerals:
   Numbers 1-10: 一，二，三，四，五，六，七，八，九，十
   Numbers 11-19: 十一，十二，十三，十四，十五，十六，十七，十八，十九
   Numbers 20-100: 二十，三十，四十，五十，六十，七十，八十，九十，一百

Cultural Information 文化常识

1. In Chinese culture, family names precede given names, so when Chinese people introduce their names, they say their family names first before their given names. Also, given names are reserved for people who know each other well, such as family members and close friends. For others, it is customary to address people by their full names or family names plus titles, for example, 李老师 'Professor Li,' 陈先生 'Mr. Chen,' 王小姐 'Miss Wang.' To be respectful, such as when inquiring about an older person's name, one typically asks 您贵姓, which literally means ' What's your honorable surname' It is then up to the addressee to say his/her surname 我姓李 'My surname is Li,' optionally followed by his/her full name 叫李文 'My full name is Li Wen.'

2. When Chinese people greet each other, they usually smile and nod their head slightly in acknowledgment. Young people may also wave their hands at each other. In formal situations, people would shake each other's hands.

3. It is socially acceptable in China for people to inquire about one another's age according to their relative social status. An older person can ask a younger person's age by 你今年几岁了？'How old are you?' A younger person may ask an older person's age by 您今年多大岁数了？'How old are you?' However, under Western influence, it is less common now for Chinese to ask about each other's age, especially young women's age. An indirect way of finding out about someone's age is to ask about his/her zodiac sign: 你是属什么的？From the answer 我属…, one can guess the other's age.

4. In traditional China, each year is represented by an animal or 'a zodiac sign' for a cycle of twelve (十二生肖). The animal signs are arranged in a set order and are repeated every twelve years. They are respectively: Rat, Ox, Tiger, Hare, Dragon, Snake, Horse, Ram, Monkey, Rooster, Dog, and Boar.

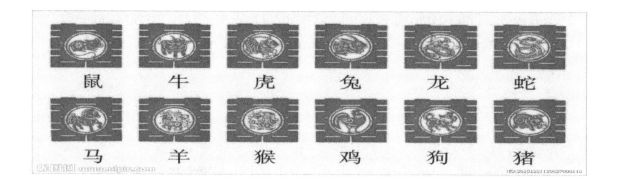

鼠　牛　虎　兔　龙　蛇

马　羊　猴　鸡　狗　猪

Pattern Drill 1 句型操练一

Substitute the underlined parts in the following sentences with the expressions in the box.

1. A: 你好！

B: 你好！

A. i. 大家好　　　ii. 同学们 (tóngxuémén, classmates)好
B. i. 老师好　　　ii. 您 (nín, you) 好

2. A: 你好吗？

B: 很好, 谢谢, 你呢？

B. i. 还好 (háihǎo, okay)
ii. 不错 (búcuò, not bad)
iii. 马马虎虎 (mǎmǎhūhū, so so)

3. A: 你叫什么名字？

B: 我叫... 你呢？

A. i. 您贵姓 (guìxìng, surname)　ii. 怎么 (zěnme, how) 称呼(chēnghu, address)您
B. i. 我姓..., 叫...　　　　　　ii. 叫我... 好了

4. A: 你是属什么的？

   B: 我是属<u>猴</u>的。

鼠 (shǔ)	牛 (niú)	虎 (hǔ)	兔 (tù)	龙 (lóng)	蛇 (shé)
马 (mǎ)	羊 (yáng)	猴 (hóu)	鸡 (jī)	狗 (gǒu)	猪 (zhū)

5. A: 你<u>几岁</u>了？

   B: 我今年<u>十九岁</u>。

> A: 多大(duōdà, how old)
>
> B. i. 十八岁
>
>   ii. 二十岁
>
>   iii. 二十二岁

6. A: 你是学什么专业的？

   B: 我学<u>商</u>.

医	工程	文学	历史	美术	化学	物理	经济	心理	数学	计算机

7. A: 你是大学几(jǐ, how many)年级学生？

   B: 我是<u>大学一年级</u>学生。

> B. i. 大学二年级/大二
>
>   ii · 大学三年级/大三
>
>   iii. 大学四年级/大四

Pattern Drill 2 句型操练二

Match each question with the response that best answers it.

1. 您贵姓？	___a. 我属虎。
2. 你今年多大？	___b. 我学工程。
3. 你是属什么的?	___c. 三年级学生。
4. 你学什么专业？	___d. 我姓李。
5. 你是大学几年级学生?	___f. 我今年二十一岁。

Pronunciation Drill 1 语音操练一

Say the following tongue twister as fast as you can, paying attention to the distinction between retroflex *shì* with the non-retroflex *sì.*

四是四，十是十。　　　　sì shì sì, shí shì shí

十四是十四，四十是四十。　shí sì shì shí sì, sì shí shì sì shí

Pronunciation Drill 2 语音操练二

Recite the classical poem 一去二三里 with the help of *pinyin.*

一去二三里，　　　yī qù èr sān lǐ

烟村四五家，　　　yān cūn sì wǔ jiā

亭台六七座，　　　tíng tái liù qī zuò

八九十枝花。　　　bā jiǔ shí zhī huā

Exercises 练习

1. Mark the tones for the following words and expressions, paying attention to tone sandhi.

1) nihao	3) yiding	5) nimen	7) bu dui
你好	一定	你们	不对

2) henhao   4) yiqi   6) women   8) bu hao

很好   一起   我们   不好

2. Write the Chinese characters that correspond to the following *pinyin*.

    1) zìjǐ   3) jièshào   5) míngzi   7) xuéshēng

    2) rènshi   4) gāoxìng   6) dàjiā   8) zhǔxiū

3. Guess the meaning and sound of the following characters by breaking them down to their respective semantic and phonetic parts.

    1) 喉 = _____ + _____ sound: _____ meaning: _____

    2) 他 = _____ + _____ sound: _____ meaning: _____

    3) 妳 = _____ + _____ sound: _____ meaning: _____

    4) 记 = _____ + _____ sound: _____ meaning : _____

4. Use each of the following characters to form two compound words and then write a sentence for each of the compound words.

    For example: 自 <u>自我</u>   <u>我来自我介绍一下。</u>

                <u>自己</u>   <u>我自己学中文。</u>

    1) 学   _____   _____

            _____   _____

    2) 年   _____   _____

            _____   _____

    3) 名   _____   _____

            _____   _____

    4) 大   _____   _____

            _____   _____

13

5. Fill in the blanks with the words given, using each word only once.

1) 自我　自己

你来介绍一下你＿＿＿＿＿＿吧。

你来＿＿＿＿＿＿介绍一下吧。

2) 专业　主修

我的＿＿＿＿＿＿是商学。

我＿＿＿＿＿＿商学。

3) 呢　吧　呀

A: 你是大一学生＿＿＿＿？

B: 是＿＿＿＿, 你＿＿＿＿？

4) 属　叫　姓

大家好！我＿＿＿＿李，＿＿＿＿李文，＿＿＿＿马。

6. Translate the following sentences into Chinese.

1) I am twenty years old.
2) I major in medical science.
3) Pleased to meet you.
4) What's your name?
5) What's your Zodiac sign?
6) What's your major?

7. Correct mistakes in the following sentences.

1) 我的姓是李
2) 我是属虎。
3) 我是很高兴认识你。
4) 什么是你的名字？
5) 你是学什么专业？
6) 我是十八岁。我是大一。

8. Write a short paragraph (50 or more characters) to your teacher, introducing yourself in Chinese. Please include the following information: greeting, your name, Chinese zodiac sign, age, year in college, major, and how you feel about learning Chinese.

9. Find out the following information about your Chinese name: how to write it in Chinese characters, the meaning of your given name, who gave you the name and why they chose this name for you. Be prepared to share this information with your classmates.

Character Stroke Order 生字笔画

亻 夕 夕 夕 名 名 97

丶 丷 宀 宁 字

乚 女 女 女 妌 姓 姓

丨 冂 曰 旦 早 早 昰 是

一 ナ 大

十 二

丨 冂 口 叮 叮 叮 呢 呢

丶 丷 丷 丷 学 学 学 学

丿 ヒ 牛 生 生

コ ヨ 尸 尸 尸 尸 居 居 属 属 属 属

亻 犭 犭 犭 狆 狌 狌 狌 猴 猴

丶 亻 冇 白 白 的 的 的

フ 又 又 对 对

16

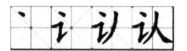

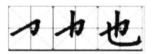

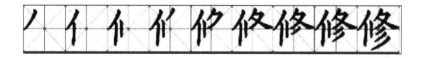

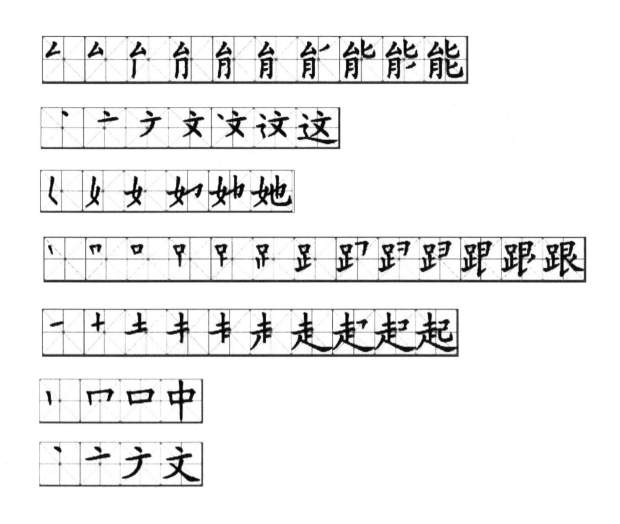

ㄥ ㄥ ㄅ 台 台 台 台 能 能 能

丶 亠 亠 文 文 这 这

乚 女 女 如 她 她

丶 口 口 卩 卩 卩 卫 趴 趴 趴 跟 跟 跟

一 十 土 キ キ 走 走 起 起 起

丶 口 口 中

丶 亠 亠 文

19

Lesson 2 第二课 My Family 我的家

Think and Share 想想说说

1. 中国人一般按照什么顺序来介绍自己家人？What is the usual order in which Chinese people introduce their family members?
2. 中国人怎么样确定他们的祖籍？How do Chinese determine the place of their family origin?
3. 中国人一般怎样回答恭维话？How do Chinese generally respond to compliments?

Dialogue 对话

陈凯文：丽莉，你家有几口人？

王丽莉：我家有五口人：爸爸，妈妈，哥哥，姐姐，和我。你呢？

陈凯文：我家有七口人：爷爷，奶奶，爸爸，妈妈，弟弟，妹妹，和我。

王丽莉：你的爸爸妈妈是做什么工作的？

陈凯文：我爸爸是开餐馆的，妈妈是会计。你呢？

王丽莉：我爸爸是电脑工程师，妈妈是老师。

陈凯文：你的哥哥姐姐是做什么的？

王丽莉：我哥哥是研究生，主修商业管理。我姐姐是护士。你呢？

陈凯文：我弟弟念中学十年级，妹妹念小学五年级。

王丽莉：你家是广东人吗？

陈凯文：是的，我父母是广东台山人。你父母是从哪里来的？

王丽莉：我父母是从台湾来的。

陈凯文：难怪你的中文说得这么好。

王丽莉：哪里，我还有很多东西要学呢。

Answer Questions 回答问题

1. 王丽莉家有几口人？How many people are there in Lily Wang's family?
2. 她们家都有些什么人？Who are there in her family?
3. 她的爸爸、妈妈是做什么工作的？What do her father and mother do for a living?

4. 她们家是从哪里来的？ Where is her family from?
5. 陈凯文家呢？ How about Kevin Chen's family?

Vocabulary 生词

1. 家	jiā	n/m	family; home; (measure word for family-own business)
2. 有	yǒu	v	to have
3. 几	jǐ	nu	how many; several
4. 口	kǒu	n/m	mouth; (measure word for number of people in a family)
5. 人	rén	n	person; people
6. 爸爸	bàba	n	dad
7. 妈妈	māma	n	mom
8. 哥哥	gēge	n	older brother
9. 姐姐	jiějie	n	older sister
10. 和	hé	conj	and
11. 爷爷	yéye	n	grandpa (on the father's side)
12. 奶奶	nǎinai	n	grandma (on the father's side)
13. 弟弟	dìdi	n	younger brother
14. 妹妹	mèimei	n	younger sister
15. 做	zuò	v	to do
16. 工作	gōngzuò	n	job
17. 开	kāi	v	to open; to operate
18. 餐馆	cānguǎn	n	restaurant
19. 会计	kuàijì	n	accountant

21

20.	电脑	diànnǎo	n	computer
21.	工程师	gōngchéngshī	n	engineer
22.	老师	lǎoshī	n	teacher
23.	研究生	yánjiūshēng	n	graduate student
24.	商业	shāngyè	n	business; commerce
25.	管理	guǎnlǐ	v/n	to manage; management
26.	护士	hùshi	n	nurse
27.	在	zài	prep/part	at (a place); (progressive particle)
28.	中学	zhōngxué	n	secondary school
29.	念	niàn	v	to attend school; to study; to read aloud
30.	小学	xiǎoxué	n	primary school
31.	父母	fùmǔ	n	parent
32.	从	cóng	prep	from
33.	哪里	nǎli	pron/idiom	where; (polite response to compliment)
34.	难怪	nánguài	idiom	no wonder
35.	说	shuō	v	to speak
36.	得	de	part	(to introduce a degree complement)
37.	这么	zhème	adv	so, such
38.	还	hái	adv	still; also
39.	多	duō	adj	many; much
40.	东西	dōngxī	n	thing; stuff
41.	要	yào	v/aux	to want; to need; to be going to

Proper Nouns 专有名词

1. 广东   guǎngdōng   Guangdong

2. 台山   táishān   Taishan

3. 台湾   táiwān   Taiwan

Map of China 中国地图

Short Reading 阅读短文

　　我的家有七口人：爷爷、奶奶、爸爸、妈妈、弟弟、妹妹、和我。我的爷爷奶奶已经退休了，跟我们住在一起。他们早年从广东移民到香港，又从香港来到美国。我们家在中国城开了一家中国餐馆，爸爸是餐馆老板，妈妈是会计，我和弟弟妹妹都是学生。

Answer Questions 回答问题

1. 作者的家有几口人？How many people are there in the writer's family?
2. 他家都有些什么人？Who are the people in his family?
3. 他的爸爸、妈妈是做什么工作的？What does his father and mother do?
4. 他们家是从哪里来的？Where is his family from?

Vocabulary 生词

1. 已经	yǐjing	adv	already
2. 退休	tuìxiū	v	to retire
3. 了	le	part	(to indicate change of situation)
4. 住	zhù	v	to reside; to live
5. 早年	zǎonián	adv	long ago
6. 移民	yímín	v/n	to immigrate; immigrant
7. 到	dào	v /prep	to arrive; to reach; to
8. 又	yòu	adv	again (in the past)
9. 们	men	pron	(plural suffix for personal pronouns)
10. 老板	lǎobǎn	n	boss
11. 都	dōu	adv	all; both

Proper Nouns 专有名词

1. 中国城	zhōngguóchéng	Chinatown
2. 香港	xiānggǎng	Hong Kong
3. 美国	měiguó	the United States of America
4. 中国	zhōngguó	China

Supplementary Vocabulary 补充生词

1. 广州	guǎngzhōu	Guangzhou
2. 福州	fúzhōu	Fuzhou
3. 温州	wēnzhōu	Wenzhou
4. 上海	shànghǎi	Shanghai
5. 北京	běijīng	Beijing

亲戚关系图

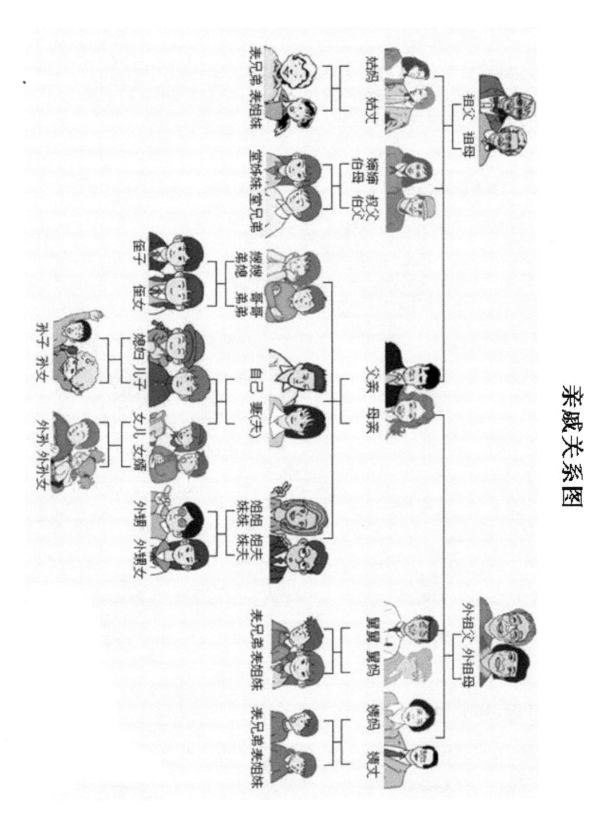

25

Task 1 Pair Activity 双人活动

Find a partner and interview each other about his/her family. Please find out the following information about your partner's family: number of people in the family, their occupations, and the place of their family origin.

Task 2 Group Activity 小组活动

Form groups of four and introduce your partner's family to your group.

Task 3 Individual Activity 个人活动

Draw a tree of your extended family with your grandparents on the top, your parents' generation in the middle, and your generation at the bottom. Label each family member by their proper terms in Chinese. You may need the following supplementary vocabulary:

1.	外公	wàigōng	grandpa (on the mother's side)
2.	外婆	wàipó	grandma (on the mother's side)
3.	伯伯	bóbo	older uncle (on the father's side)
4.	叔叔	shūshu	younger uncle (on the father's side)
5.	姑妈、姑姑	gūmā gūgu	aunt (on the father's side)
6.	舅舅	jiùjiu	uncle (on the mother's side)
7.	姨妈、姨姨	yímā yíyi	aunt (on the mother's side)
8.	堂哥、弟、姐、妹	tánggē dì jiě mèi	cousin with the same family as yours
9.	表哥、弟、姐、妹	biǎogē dì jiě mèi	cousin with a different family
10.	兄弟姐妹	xiōngdìjiěmèi	siblings

Task 4 Pair Activity 双人活动

Show your family tree to your partner and tell him/her about your extended family.

Character Notes 汉字讲解

1. 父字头

The 'paternal radical' implies 'father' or 'grandfather.' For example:

爸爸	bàba	n	dad
爷爷	yéye	n	grandpa (on the father's side)

2. 禾木旁

The 'seed radical' implies 'planting.' For example:

和	hé	conj	and
程	chéng	n	process
移	yí	v/n	to move

3. 又字旁

The 'again radical' classifies a group of words whose shared properties are unclear now. For example:

对	duì	adj	correct
难	nán	adj	difficult

4. 走之旁

The "walk zigzag radical' implies 'walking' or 'distance.' For example:

这	zhè	pron	this
还	hái	adv	still; to return
退	tuì	v	to retreat

Grammar and Usage 语法讲解

1. 的 here is used after a noun or a pronoun to form possessive in Chinese, for example, 我的 'my.' When talking about one's family, 的 may be omitted, for example, 我家 'my family,' 你父母 'your parents,' 她兄弟姐妹 'her siblings.'

2. In Chinese, a measure word must be used between a numeral (as well as demonstrative pronouns 这 'this,' 那 'that,' or 哪 'which') and a noun to indicate the shape, size or quantity of the noun, for example, 四口人 'four people (in a family),' 一家餐馆 'one restaurant,' etc.

3. 得 is used after an action verb to introduce a degree complement or the manner in which the action is conducted. For example, in 你的中文说得这么好 'You speak Chinese so well,' 得 introduces the degree complement 这么好 'so well' to modify the verb 说 'to speak.' Taken together, V +得+ Adj describes the manner in which the action is done. For example:
   1) 她们玩得很高兴。They played happily.
   2) 我家住得很近。 My family lives close by.

4. 了 is a particle used at the end of a verb to indicate a change in situation. For example:
   1) 我的爷爷奶奶已经退休了。My grandparents have already retired. (They used to work.)
   2) 我家在中国城开了一家中国餐馆。 My family has opened a Chinese restaurant in Chinatown. (We didn't use to own a restaurant.)

Cultural Information 文化常识

1. In Chinese culture, it is customary to introduce the older male family member first before the female counterpart, for example, 爷爷 before 奶奶，爸爸 before 妈妈，哥哥 before 姐姐, 弟弟 before 妹妹.

2. Chinese people trace their family origin (祖籍) to the birthplace of their grandfather on the father's side. Therefore, they consider themselves as originated from that place even if they have never been to the place themselves. For example, a person can call himself/herself Cantonese if his/her father or grandfather is originally from the province of Guangdong, whether he/she has been to Guangdong or not.

3. Chinese rarely accept compliments with a straight 'thank you' as Americans do. To show modesty, they typically reject or denigrate the compliments by saying things like 哪里 'not at all', 没有了 'not really', followed by some explanations why they don't deserve the compliments.

4. 中国城, also known as 唐人街, are ethnic enclaves for overseas Chinese found in many urban centers throughout the world. Populated mostly by Chinese immigrants throughout history, Chinatowns have served as centers of commerce and tourism for ethnic Chinese and non-Chinese alike. Some Chinatowns such as those in New York City and San Francesco are viable industrial and residential communities with garment factories, apartment buildings, schools, places of worship, parks, hospitals along with shops, restaurants, and etc.

Pattern Drill 1 句型操练一

Substitute the underlined parts in the following sentences with the expressions in the box.

1. A: 你家有几口人？

  B: 我家有<u>五口人：爸爸，妈妈，哥哥，姐姐，和我</u>。

> B. i. 三口人：妈妈，妹妹和我
>
>   ii. 四口人：爸爸，妈妈，弟弟，和我。
>
>   iii. 六口人：爸爸，妈妈，哥哥，姐姐，弟弟，妹妹和我。

2. A: 你有几个兄弟姐妹？

  B: 我有<u>一个哥哥，一个妹妹</u>。

> B. i. 两个哥哥
>
>   ii. 三个姐姐
>
>   iii. 我没有兄弟姐妹

3. A： 你的父母是做什么工作的？

  B： 我爸爸是<u>开餐馆的</u>，妈妈是<u>会计</u>。

> B. i. 工程师　老师
>
>   ii. 商人　　研究生
>
>   iii. 老师　　护士

4. A： 你家是<u>广东人</u>吗？

  B： 是的，我父母是从<u>广东</u>来的。

A. i. 上海人	B. i. 上海
ii. 温州人	ii. 温州
iii. 福州人	iii. 福州
iv. 广州人	iv. 广州
v. 北京人	v. 北京

Pattern Drill 2 句型操练二

Match each question with the response that best answers it.

1. 你的哥哥是做什么工作的？	___a. 不，我家是香港人。
2. 你家是广东人吗？	___b. 我父母是从福州来的。
3. 你家有几口人？	___c. 我妈妈是工程师。
4. 你父母是从哪里来的？	___d. 他是研究生。
5. 你妈妈是老师吗？	___e. 我家有四口人，爸爸，妈妈，姐姐和我。

Pronunciation Drill 1 语音操练一

Pronounce the following pairs of words, paying attention to the final nasals.

1) gōngchéng	工程	3) fēngshuǐ	风水	5) rénmín	人民
gōngchén	功臣	fēnshuǐ	分水	rènmìng	认命
2) chōngfèn	充分	4) chénnián	陈年	6) míngzi	名字
chūnfēn	春分	chéngnián	成年	mínzhì	民治

Pronunciation Drill 2 语音操练二

Recite the classical poem 静夜思 by 李白 with the help of *pinyin*.

床前明月光，	chuáng qián míng yuè guāng
疑是地上霜。	yí shì dì shàng shuāng
举头望明月，	jǔ tóu wàng míng yuè
低头思故乡。	dī tóu sī gù xiāng

Exercises 练习

1. Write the Chinese characters that correspond to the following *pinyin*.

    1) cānguǎn   3) diànnǎo   5) gōngchéng   7) yánjiū

    2) tuìxiū   4) yímín   6) nánguài   8) lǎobǎn

2. Guess the meaning and sound of the following characters by breaking them down to their respective semantic and phonetic parts.

    1) 爹 = _____ + _____ sound: _____ meaning: _____

    2) 种 = _____ + _____ sound: _____ meaning: _____

    3) 叔 = _____ + _____ sound: _____ meaning: _____

    4) 达 = _____ + _____ sound: _____ meaning: _____

3. Use each of the following characters to form two compound words and then write a sentence for each of the compound words.

    1) 人   _____   _____

          _____   _____

2) 做 _____ _____

_____ _____

3) 好 _____ _____

_____ _____

4) 开 _____ _____

_____ _____

4. Fill in the blanks with the following words.

1) 做　　工作

A：你的姐姐是_____什么_____的？

B：她是会计。

2) 爷爷　外公

妈妈的爸爸叫_____，　爸爸的爸爸叫_____。

3) 舅舅　伯伯　叔叔

爸爸的哥哥叫_____，　爸爸的弟弟叫_____，妈妈的哥哥、弟弟

都叫_____。

4) 是的　哪里

A：你家是从台湾来的吗？

B：_____，我家是从台湾来的。你是_____人？

5. Translate the following sentences into Chinese.

1) How many people are there in your family?
2) Do your grandparents (on your father's side) live with your family?
3) What do your parents do (for a living)?
4) My parents have already retired.
5) Do you have any siblings (兄弟姐妹)?
6) Where is your family from

6. Correct mistakes in the following sentences.

   1）你家有几多人？
   2）你是作什么的？
   3）我念一年级大学。
   4）我的爷爷奶奶住在一起跟我们。
   5）他们早年是移民来美国的。
   6）我们家开了一家中餐馆在中国城.

7. Write a short paragraph (50 or more characters) about your family. Please introduce your family members, their occupations, and the place of your family's origin.

8. Find out the following information about your Chinese name: how to write it in Chinese characters, the meaning of your given name, who gave you the name and why they chose this name for you. Be prepared to share this information with your classmates.

Character Stroke Order 生字笔画

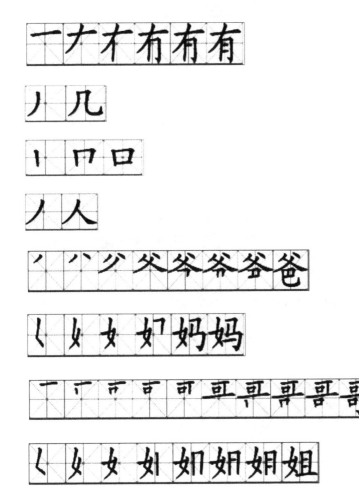

33

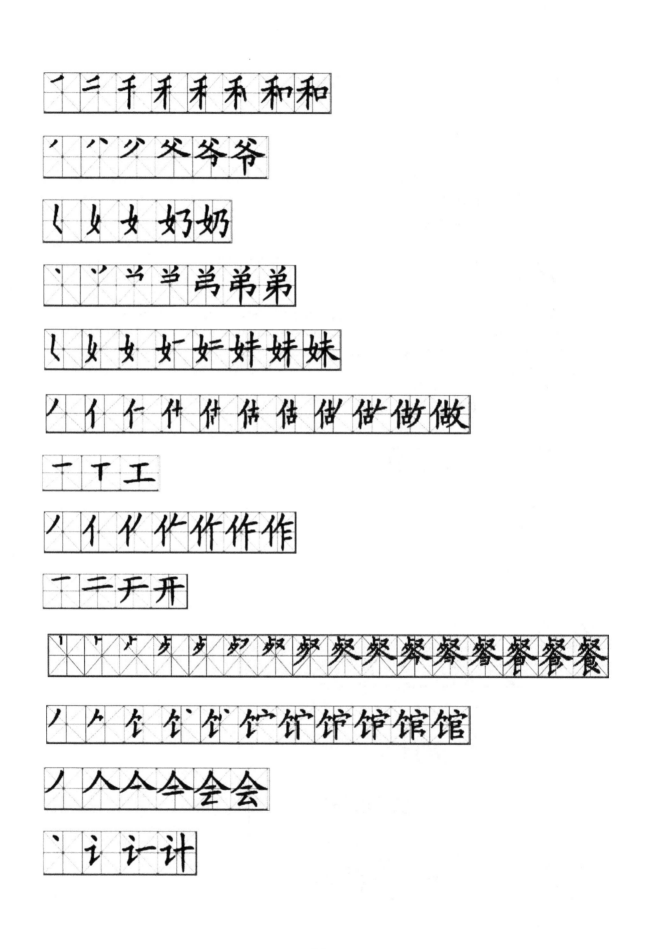

一 二 千 禾 禾 禾 和 和

丿 八 少 父 爷 爷

く 女 女 奶 奶

丷 宀 弟 弟 弟

く 女 女 奻 奻 姝 妹 妹

丿 亻 仁 什 件 估 估 做 做 做

一 丁 工

丿 亻 化 作 作 作 作

一 二 于 开

丿 夕 夕 夕 夕 夕 怒 怒 怒 餐 餐 餐 餐 餐

丿 夕 夕 饣 饣 饣 饣 馆 馆 馆

丿 人 仝 仝 会 会

丶 讠 计 计

丨 冂 冂 日 电

丿 刀 月 月 肜 胪 胪 胶 脑 脑

一 二 千 禾 禾 禾 秆 秆 秆 程 程

丨 丿 丿 厂 厂 炉 师

一 十 土 耂 考 老

一 丆 丆 石 石 矿 矿 砑 研

丶 丷 宀 宀 宑 宊 究

丿 𥫗 𥫗 𥫗 𥫗 竺 竺 竺 竽 笲 笲 筦 管 管

一 二 干 王 珇 珇 玗 玴 理 理 理

一 十 才 扌 护 护 护

一 十 士

一 ナ 才 右 在 在

丿 人 仝 今 今 念 念 念

亅 小 小

八 八 父 父

ㄥ 母 母 母 母

丿 人 从 从

丨 口 口 叩 吗 吗 咽 哪 哪

丨 口 曰 旦 甲 甲 里

丿 又 双 对 对 难 难 难 难

忄 忄 忄 忄 怪 怪 怪 怪

讠 讠 讠 讠 讠 说 说 说

彳 彳 彳 彳 彳 彳 得 得 得

一 丆 不 不 不 还 还

勹 勹 夕 多 多 多

一 东 车 车 东

一 丅 丙 丙 两 西

一 丅 丙 两 西 西 要 要 要

36

コ コ 已

乙 纟 纟 纠 纵 纶 纶 经

コ コ ヨ 巨 艮 艮 艮 退 退

丿 亻 仁 什 休 休

了 了

丿 亻 亻 亻 作 住 住

丨 冂 日 旦 旦 早

一 二 千 禾 禾 禾 移 移 移 移 移

コ コ 尺 艮 民

一 工 五 万 至 至 到 到

フ 又

丿 亻 亻 们 们

一 十 才 木 朳 朳 板 板

一 十 土 耂 者 者 者 者 都

37

Unit Two 第二单元

My College Life 我的大学生活

Lesson 3 第三课 My College 我的大学

Think and Share 想想说说

1. 你这个学期选了几门课？How many classes are you taking this semester?
2. 你都选了些什么课？What are the classes you are taking?
3. 你毕业以后想做什么？为什么? What do you want to do when you graduate? Why?
4. 你有什么爱好？What are your hobbies?

Dialogue 对话

王丽莉：凯文，你这个学期选了几门课？

陈凯文：我这个学期选了六门课。

王丽莉：你为什么选这么多课？

陈凯文：因为我想快点毕业、早点工作。

王丽莉：那你都选了些什么课呢？

陈凯文：数学、经济学、会计学、历史、文学、还有中文。你呢？

王丽莉：我只选了五门课：数学、化学、生物学、音乐、和中文。

陈凯文：你喜欢音乐？

王丽莉：是呀，我爱唱歌、弹钢琴。你呢？

陈凯文：我喜欢打篮球、玩电子游戏。

王丽莉：那什么时候，我们一起去打篮球、唱 KTV，好吗？

陈凯文：好呀，一言为定。

Answer Questions 回答问题

1. 陈凯文这个学期选了几门课？How many classes did Kevin Chen take this semester?
2. 他都选了些什么课？What classes did he take?
3. 他为什么选这么多课？Why did he take so many classes?
4. 他有什么爱好? What are his hobbies?
5. 王丽莉这个学期选了几门课？How many classes did Lily Wang take this semester?
6. 她都选了些什么课？What classes did she take?
7. 她有什么爱好？What are her hobbies?

Vocabulary 生词

1.	生活	shēnghuó	n/v	life; to live
2.	个	gè	m	(generic measure word)
3.	学期	xuéqī	n	semester
4.	选	xuǎn	v	to select
5.	门	mén	m	(measure word for school subjects)
6.	课	kè	n	school subject; lesson
7.	(一)些	(yì)xiē	a/adv	some; unspecified number
8.	为什么	wèishénme	pron	why
9.	因为	yīnwèi	conj	because
10.	想	xiǎng	v	to want; to think
11.	快点	kuàidiǎn	adv	faster
12.	毕业	bìyè	v/n	to graduate; graduation
13.	早点	zǎodiǎn	adv	earlier
14.	那	nà	conj/pron	in that case; that
15.	数学	shùxué	n	math
16.	经济学	jīngjìxué	n	economics
17.	会计学	kuàijìxué	n	accounting
18.	历史	lìshǐ	n	history
19.	文学	wénxué	n	literature
20.	还有	háiyǒu	conj	also
21.	只	zhǐ	adv	only
22.	化学	huàxué	n	chemistry

23. 生物学	shēngwùxué	n	biology
24. 音乐	yīnyuè	n	music
25. 喜欢	xǐhuan	v	to like
26. 爱	ài	v	to love
27. 唱歌	chànggē	v	to sing
28. 弹	tán	v	to play (musical instrument)
29. 钢琴	gāngqín	n	piano
30. 打	dǎ	v	to play (ball); to hit;
31. 篮球	lánqiú	n	basketball
32. 玩	wán	v	to play (game); to have fun
33. 电子	diànzǐ	a	electronic
34. 游戏	yóuxì	n	games
电子游戏	diànzǐyóuxì	n	video games
35. 时候	shíhou	n	time,when
什么时候	shénmeshíhou	adv	what time; one of these days
36. 去	qù	v	to go
37. 一言为定	yìyánwéidìng	idiom	it's a deal; a promise is a promise

Short Reading 阅读短文

我的学校在一座大学城里边，校园很大也很美。除了有教学楼和图书馆以外，还有体育馆和学生活动中心，里边有餐厅、商店、礼堂、健身房、游泳池、球场等等。除了楼房以外，校园里边到处都是绿草坪。我很喜欢我的学校。

Answer Questions 回答问题

1. 作者的学校在哪里？Where is the writer's school?

41

2. 校园怎么样？为什么？How is the campus? Why?

3. 体育馆里边都有些什么？What are there in the gymnasium?

4. 学生活动中心里边都有些什么？What are there in the Student Activity Center?

Vocabulary 生词

1.	学校	xuéxiào	n	school
2.	座	zuò	m	(measure word for town or building)
3.	大学城	dàxuéchéng	n	college town
4.	里边	lǐbian	n	inside
5.	校园	xiàoyuán	n	campus
6.	大	dà	a	big,; large
7.	美	měi	a	beautiful
8.	除了…以外	chúle… yǐwài	prep	except; besides
9.	教学楼	jiàoxuélóu	n	classroom building
10.	图书馆	túshūguǎn	n	library
11.	体育馆	tǐyùguǎn	n	gymnasium
12.	活动	huódòng	n	activity
13.	中心	zhōngxīn	n	center
14.	餐厅	cāntīng	n	cafeteria
15.	商店	shāngdiàn	n	shop; store
16.	礼堂	lǐtáng	n	auditorium
17.	健身房	jiànshēnfáng	n	fitness room
18.	游泳池	yóuyǒngchí	n	swimming pool
19.	球场	qiúchǎng	n	ball court

20. 等等	děngděng	part	and so on; and so forth; etc.
21. 楼房	lóufáng	n	building
22. 到处	dàochù	n	everywhere
23. 绿	lǜ	adj	green
24. 草坪	cǎopíng	n	lawn

Task 1 Group Activity 小组活动

Talk about your classes, your career goals, and your hobbies with your group members.

Task 2 Individual Activity 个人活动

Draw a map of your campus, labeling in Chinese its main buildings such as the administration building (行政主楼), classroom buildings (by department 系), student activity center, gymnasium, cafeterias, dorms (宿舍楼) and etc.

Task 3 Pair Activity 双人活动

Role-play the following situations with a partner in 4 or 5 sentences each. You are a new student looking for a particular place on campus. Ask for directions from another student you happen to encounter. Please feel free to use the map you have drawn as a prop. You may optionally present this skit to the whole class.

Characters Notes 汉字讲解

1. 三点水

The 'three drop water radical' implies 'water.' For example:

活	huó	adj/v	alive; to live
济	jì	v	to cross rivers; to aid
游泳池	yóuyǒngchí	n/v	swim
池	chí	n	pool

2. 两点水

The 'two drop water radical' implies 'ice' or 'cold.' For example:

冰	bīng	n	ice
冷	lěng	a	cold
冲	chōng	v	to rinse

准	zhǔn		a certain

3. 提土旁

The 'dirt radical' implies 'ground.' For example:

城	chéng	n	town
场	chǎng	n	field
坪	píng	n	lawn
堂	táng	n	hall

4. 木字旁

The 'wood radical' implies 'tree' or 'wood.' For example:

校	xiào	n	school
楼	lóu	n	building

Grammar and Usage 语法讲解

1. 都 is an adverb placed before a verb to indicate 'all,' 'both,' or 'exactly.' It usually goes with indefinite pronouns or adverbs such as 些 'some', 什么 'what', 到处 'everywhere', etc. For example:

   1) 你都选了些什么课？What classes did you choose *exactly*?

   2) 我的弟弟、妹妹都是学生。*Both* my younger brother and sister are students.

   3) 你家都有些什么人？Who are *all* the people in your family?

   4) 校园里到处都是绿草坪。There is green lawn *everywhere* on campus.

2. 在...里边 is a prepositional phrased used around a noun phrase to indicate the location of 'inside...' Here are some similar expressions for locations:

   在...外边   outside...

   在...上边   on...; above...

   在...下边   below...

   在...左边   on the left of...

   在...右边   on the right of...

   在...东、南、西、北边   on the east, south, west, and north side of...

44

3. 也 is an adverb meaning 'also' or 'too.' It is used to add adjective or a verb phrase to form a parallel structure 'both...and...' For example:

1) 校园很大也很美。The campus is both big and pretty
2) 我的家很大也很好。My home is both big and nice.
3) 我爱唱歌也爱弹钢琴。I love both singing and playing the piano.
4) 我喜欢打台球，也喜欢玩电子游戏。 I like to play pool and video games.

Notice the difference between 也 and 和. 也 is used to combine adjectives or verb phrases whereas 和 is used to combine pronouns and noun phrases. For example:

1) 我家很大也很好。My family is big and good. *我家很大和很好。
2) 我爱唱歌和弹钢琴。I love singing and playing the piano.*我爱唱歌和爱弹钢琴。

4. 除了...(以外) is a prepositional phrase used around a noun phrase to mean 'except' or 'besides.' It is usually followed by 还 'still' or 也 'also' plus a verb in the next sentence. For example,

1) 除了音乐(以外)，你还喜欢什么？Besides music, what else do you like?
2) 我们家除了我以外，我弟弟也在学中文。In my family, in addition to me, my younger brother is also learning Chinese.

Cultural Information 文化常识

1. KTV, commonly known as 'karaoke' or 卡拉 OK, is a popular form of interactive entertainment in Asia and Asian American communities in North America. It is said to be originated from Japan, where amateurs as well as professional musicians sang on the stage along with a musical accompaniment recorded on cassette tapes. Today, karaoke is often found in 'karaoke boxes' in Asia, where patrons pay a fee to sing along with pre-recorded musical accompaniment as the lead vocalist for entertainment. It is also found in many restaurants, bars, and lounges throughout the world where people sing in public into a microphone and karaoke equipment and socialize.

2. 大学城 'college town' refers to a community dominated by the presence of a college or university. In most college towns in America, the college or the university may be at the center of the town's economic and social lives, with most of the businesses in town catering to the needs of the college or the university. In some small American college towns, the student population may outnumber that of the local residents. Nowadays, with urban development, more and more colleges and universities in

China are moving to the suburbs, creating satellite college towns with a cluster of colleges and universities in one place.

Pattern Drill 1 句型操练一

Substitute the underlined parts in the following sentences with phrases in the box.

1. A: 你这个学期选了几门课？

   B: 我这个学期选了<u>六门</u>课。

B. i. 四门课
ii. 五门课
iii. 七门课

2. A: 你都选了什么课？

   B: <u>数学、经济学、会计学、历史、文学、还有中文</u>。

B. i. 数学、历史、文学、还有中文
ii. 化学、数学、生物，还有物理
iii. 音乐、美术、化学、还有心理学
iv. 体育、计算机、会计学和经济学

3. A: 你喜欢<u>音乐</u>？

   B: 是的。 我爱<u>唱歌、弹钢琴</u>。

A. i. 音乐	B. i. 中国音乐、美国音乐
B. ii. 玩电子游戏	ii. 玩 DS, Wii, Xbox
iii. 体育	iii. 打球、游泳

Pattern Drill 2 句型操练二

Match each question with the response that best answers it.

1. 你喜欢音乐？	___a. 数学、历史、文学、还有中文。
2. 你都选了什么课？	___b. 因为我想快点毕业、早点工作。
3. 你这个学期选了几门课？	___c. 好呀，一言为定。
4. 你为什么选这么多课？	___d. 是的。我爱唱歌、弹钢琴。
5. 我们一起去中国城打台球,好吗？	___c. 我这个学期选了六门课.。

Pronunciation Drill 语音操练

Recite and sing the lyric of a popular Chinese folk song 茉莉花 with the help of *pinyin* .

好一朵美丽的茉莉花	Hǎo yī duǒ měilìde mòlihuā
好一朵美丽的茉莉花	Hǎo yīduǒ měilìde mòlihuā
芬芳美丽满枝桠	Fēnfāng měilì mǎn zhīyā
又香又白人人夸	Yòu xiāng yòu bái rénrén kuā
让我来将你摘下	Ràng wǒ lái jiāng nǐ zhāixià
送给别人家	Sònggěi biérén jiā
茉莉花呀茉莉花	Mòlihuā yā mòlihuā

Exercises 练习

1. Write the Chinese characters that correspond to the words in *pinyin* below.

1) xuéqī 3) yóuxì 5) xǐhuan 7) yìyánwéidìng

2) ài 4) cāntīng 6) lóufáng 8) túshūguǎn

47

2. Match the words on the top line with words that typically go with them on the bottom
   line.

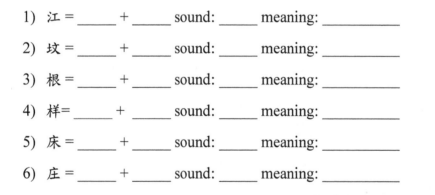

選　　　弹　　　打　　　唱　　　玩　　　一言

球　　　为定　　　游戏　　　课　　　歌　　　钢琴

3. Guess the meaning and sound of the following characters by breaking them down to
   their respective semantic and phonetic parts.

    1) 江 = _____ + _____ sound: _____ meaning: _____

    2) 坟 = _____ + _____ sound: _____ meaning: _____

    3) 根 = _____ + _____ sound: _____ meaning: _____

    4) 样 = _____ + _____ sound: _____ meaning: _____

    5) 床 = _____ + _____ sound: _____ meaning: _____

    6) 庄 = _____ + _____ sound: _____ meaning: _____

4. Use each of the following characters to make two compound words and then write
   a sentence for each of the compound words.

1) 点　　_____　　_____

　　　　　_____　　_____

2) 打　　_____　　_____

　　　　　_____　　_____

3) 美　　_____　　_____

　　　　　_____　　_____

4) 边　　_____　　_____

　　　　　_____　　_____

5. Fill in the blanks with the following words, using each word only once.

1) 除了... 以外   在...里边

_____ 学生活动中心_____，有餐厅、商店、还有礼堂。

_____ 教学楼_____，还有图书馆、体育馆等等。

2) 也   和

我爱唱歌_____爱打球。

我喜欢音乐_____体育。

3) 都   只

A: 这个学期我_____选了四门课。

B: 你_____选了什么课？

A: 数学、文学、化学、跟中文。

4) 打   玩   弹

她的姐姐喜欢_____琴，哥哥爱_____球、_____游戏。

6. Translate the following sentences into Chinese.

1) No wonder you chose so many classes, because you wish to graduate sooner.
2) Of the classes I chose this semester, I like history and biology.
3) Everywhere inside the classroom buildings, there are students and teachers.
4) Except for buildings, there is green lawn everywhere on campus.
5) One of these days, let's go to Chinatown together to sing karaoke, ok?
6) Ok, it's a deal.

7. Correct mistakes in the following sentences.

1) 除了爸爸、妈妈以外，你家也有什么人？
2) 除了唱歌以外，王丽莉都喜欢弹钢琴。
3) 在学校的图书馆里边，到处还是人。
4) 我们学校的中国学生很多和很好。
5) 他主修经济学也商学。
6) 在体育馆有游泳池、健身房、还有球场。

49

8. Write a paragraph (50 or more characters) about your coursework this semester (number of courses and course titles), your future career goals, and your hobbies.

9. Tell your classmates about a university you have visited. Describe its location, its facilities, and its campus. State how you like the university and why.

Character Strok Order 生字笔画

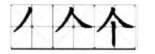

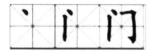

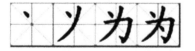

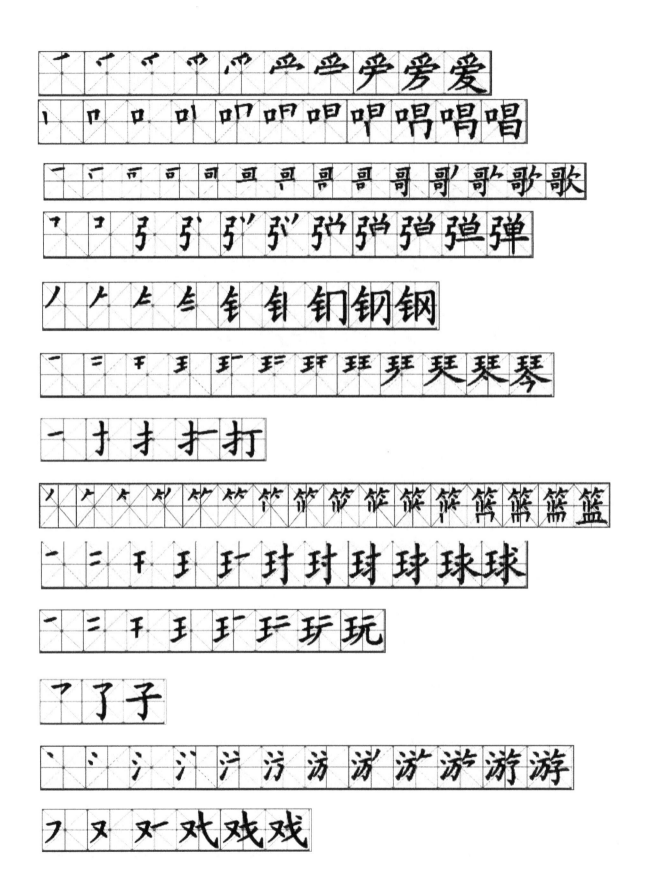

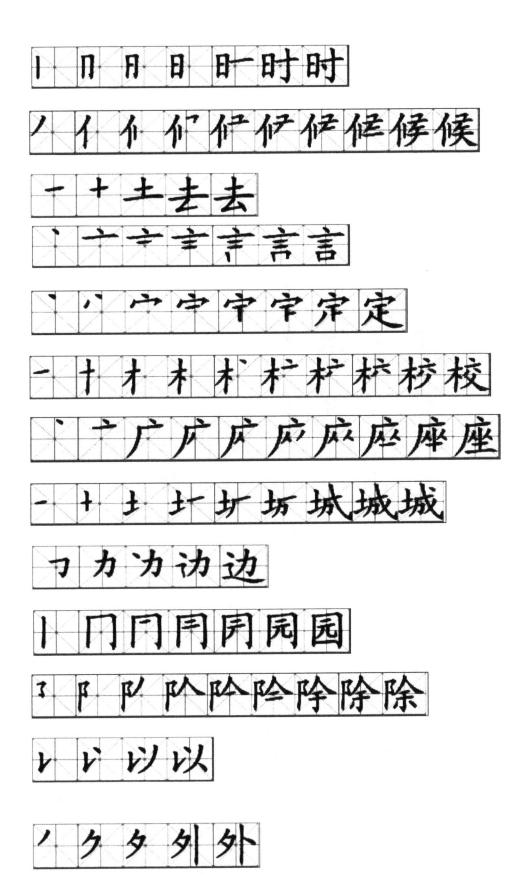

| 丨 | 冂 | 冃 | 日 | 旪 | 时 | 时 |

| 丿 | 亻 | 仃 | 伫 | 伫 | 伫 | 俟 | 候 | 候 |

| 一 | 十 | 土 | 去 | 去 |

| 丶 | 二 | 亠 | 亖 | 言 | 言 | 言 |

| 丶 | 八 | 宀 | 宀 | 宀 | 宀 | 定 | 定 |

| 一 | 十 | 才 | 木 | 杧 | 杧 | 杧 | 杧 | 杦 | 校 |

| 丶 | 亠 | 广 | 广 | 庀 | 庐 | 庐 | 座 | 座 | 座 |

| 一 | 十 | 土 | 圵 | 圻 | 坊 | 城 | 城 | 城 |

| 乛 | 力 | 办 | 边 | 边 |

| 丨 | 冂 | 冂 | 用 | 用 | 园 | 园 |

| 乛 | 阝 | 阝 | 阶 | 阶 | 除 | 除 | 除 | 除 |

| 乚 | ㇄ | 以 | 以 |

| 丿 | 夕 | 夕 | 列 | 外 |

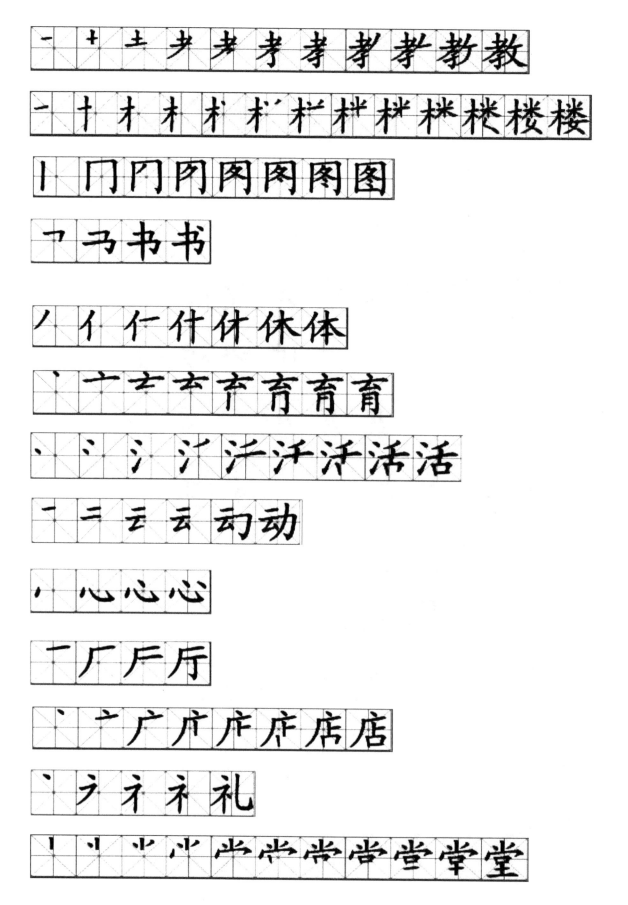

一 十 土 步 耂 孝 孝 孝 教 教

一 十 才 木 杧 杧 栌 栌 样 楼 楼 楼

丨 冂 冈 冈 图 图 图 图

フ ⼹ 书 书

丿 亻 仁 什 仕 休 体

丶 亠 古 玄 亩 育 育 育

丶 冫 氵 汀 汻 汻 汗 活 活

一 二 云 云 动 动

丶 心 心 心

一 厂 厃 厅

丶 广 广 庐 庐 店 店

丶 ⼹ 礻 礼

丨 ⺌ ⺌ ⺌ 尚 尚 堂 堂 堂 堂 堂

丿 亻 亻⁻ 亻⁻ 亻⁼ 亻⁼ 亻⁼ 律 健 健

丿 亻 亻 勹 甸 甸 身 身

丶 一 一 户 户 户 房 房

丶 丶 氵 汀 汀 汩 泳 泳

丶 丶 氵 汈 池 池

一 十 土 圬 场 场

丿 亻 亻 亇 竹 竹 竿 竿 笙 笙 等 等

丿 夕 夂 处 处

乚 乡 乡 纟 纠 纠 绀 绿 绿 绿

一 艹 艹 艹 苎 苎 苗 草 草

一 十 土 圠 圠 坪 坪 坪

Lesson 4 第四课 My Student Life 我的学生生活

Think and Share 想想说说

1. 你喜不喜欢你的学生生活？为什么？Do you like your campus life? Why?
2. 你爱不爱吃学校的饭菜？为什么？Do you like the food on campus? Why?
3. 你有没有参加过什么学生社团的活动？Have you participated in any student club activities?
4. 你想不想家？为什么？Are you home-sick? Why?

Dialogue 对话

王丽莉：嗨，凯文，你去哪里？

陈凯文：哦，你好，丽莉。我去图书馆。

王丽莉：我正好也要去图书馆，我们一起走吧。

陈凯文：好的。你经常去图书馆吗？

王丽莉：是的，我每天除了上课，就是去图书馆。你呢？

陈凯文：我也是每天三点一线：宿舍，教室，餐厅。有时也会去图书馆。

王丽莉：你喜欢吃学校的饭菜吗？

陈凯文：一点也不喜欢，没有我家的饭菜好吃。

王丽莉：对了，我差点忘了你家是开餐馆的。

陈凯文：对呀，什么时候我请你去我家的餐馆吃饭，好吗？

王丽莉：好呀，我一定去。

陈凯文：你喜欢大学生活吗？

王丽莉：还好，就是太忙了，每天除了上课，就是自习。

陈凯文：什么时候我介绍你参加一个中国学生社团，会很有意思的。

王丽莉：太好了，一言为定。

Answer Questions 回答问题

1．陈凯文在学校里每天都做什么？What does Kevin Chen do at school every day?
2．王丽莉在学校里每天都做什么？What does Lily Wang do at school every day?
3．陈凯文喜不喜欢学校餐厅的饭？为什么？Does Kevin Chen like the food in the school cafeteria? Why or why not?

4．王丽莉喜不喜欢大学生活？Does Lily Wang like her college life?
5．陈凯文要介绍王丽莉参加什么？为什么？What is Kevin Chen going to introduce Lily Wang to? Why?

Vocabulary 生词

1. 哦	ò	int	oh
2. 正好	zhènghǎo	adv	to happen to
3. 走	zǒu	v	to walk
4. 经常	jīngcháng	adv	often
5. 上课	shàngkè	v	to go to class
6. 就	jiù	adv	just
7. 每	měi	a	every
8. 天	tiān	n	day
9. 三点一线	sāndiǎnyíxiàn	idiom	to follow the same route
10. 宿舍	sùshè	n	dorm
11. 教室	jiàoshì	n	classroom
12. 有时	yǒushí	adv	sometimes
13. 吃	chī	v	to eat
14. 饭菜	fàncài	n	food; meal
15. 一点也不	yìdiǎn yě bù	idiom	not at all
16. 没(有)	méi(yǒu)	adv	not (have)
17. 好吃	hǎochī	adj	delicious
18. 对了	duìle	int	oh yes
19. 差点	chàdiǎn	adv	nearly
20. 忘	wàng	v	to forget

57

21. 请	qǐng	v	to invite; to request; please
22. 一定	yídìng	adv	certainly; definitely
23. 还好	háihǎo	idiom	it's alright
24. 太	tài	adv	too; extremely
25. 忙	máng	adj	busy
26. 自习	zìxí	v	to study by oneself
27. 参加	cānjiā	v	to join; to participate
28. 社团	shètuán	n	club; association
29. 会	huì	aux	will; know how
30. 有意思	yǒuyìsi	adj	interesting
31. 太好了	tàihǎole	idiom	great; terrific

Short Reading 阅读短文

我的大学生活很有意思，每天除了学新的东西以外，还可以交新的朋友。学校里有很多学生社团，我参加了一个中国学生社团，大家一起聊天、唱歌、打球，很开心。不过，有时我也会想家，特别想吃家里的饭菜。还有，就是钱花得太快，不到月底，钱都花光了。

Answer Questions 回答问题

1. 作者喜不喜欢他/她的大学生活？为什么？Does the writer enjoy his/her college life?
Why or why not?
2. 作者的大学里有没有中国学生社团？Are there any Chinese student clubs in the writer's university?
3. 大家在学生社团里都做些什么？What does everyone do in the student clubs?
4. 作者想不想家？为什么？Does the writer miss his/her home? Why or why not?

Vocabulary 生词

1. 新	xīn	adj	new
2. 可以	kěyǐ	aux	can; may

3.	交	jiāo	v	to make friend with; to submit
4.	朋友	péngyou	n	friend
5.	聊天	liáotiān	v	to chat
6.	开心	kāixīn	adj	happy
7.	不过	búguò	conj	but
8.	特别	tèbié	adv	especially
9.	钱	qián	n	money
10.	花	huā	v/n	to spend; flower
11.	不	bù	adv	no; not
12.	月底	yuèdǐ	n	end of the month
13.	光	guāng	a/n	used up (used after a verb as a resultative complement) ; light

Task 1 Pair Activity 双人活动

Pair up with a partner and talk about your daily routine at school.

Task 2 Pair Activity 双人活动

With a partner design a poster in Chinese to advertise a student club activity.

Task 3 Class Work 全班活动

With your partner, role-play the following situation. You are members of a student club on campus. Give a brief "sales talk" in Chinese to persuade your classmates to join your club activities. You may use the poster you designed earlier as a prop.

Poster designed by Janice Tsang and Jessica Zhang, Stony Brook University

Character Notes 汉字讲解

1. 心字旁

The 'heart radical' on the left of the character implies 'feeling' and at the bottm 'mental activitity.' For example:

快	kuài	adj	quick
忙	máng	adj	busy
想	xiǎng	v	to want; to think
忘	wàng	v	to forget
意思	yìsi	n	meaning
心	ixīn	n	heart

2. 月字旁

The 'moon radical' implies 'the moon' or 'body part.' For example:

月	yuè	n	the Moon; month
期	qī	n	period (of time)
脑	nǎo	n	brain
朋	péng	n	friend

3. 宝盖头

The 'treasure cover radical' impliesis 'treasure' or 'roof.' For example:

家	jiā	n/m	family; home; (measure word for family-own business)
宿	sù	v	to sleep through the night
室	shì	n	classroom
定	dìng	adj	fixed; certain

4. 草字头

The 'grass radical' implies 'plants.' For example:

菜	cài	n	vegetable
花	huā	n/v	flower ; to spend

Grammar and Usage 语法讲解

1. 除了...就是 is an idiomatic expression to indicate there are only two options 'either...or...' For example:

    1) 学校里的饭不好吃，除了三明治，就是汉堡包。The food on campus is not good. It's either sandwich or hamburger.

    2) 学校的生活没有意思，除了上课，就是自习。Life on campus is boring. It's either going to classes or studying by yourself.

2. 一点也 followed by a negative particle 不 or 没 is a way to negate a predicate meaning 'not at all.' It is placed directly before the predicate to be negated. For example:

    1) 我一点也不喜欢学校的饭菜。I do not like the school's food at all.

    2) 她一点也不会花钱。She does not know how to spend money.

    3) 你一点也不想家吗？Don't you miss your family at all?

    4) 学生生活一点也没有意思。Student life is not interesting at all.

3. 没有, which literally means 'do not have,' can be used in comparative sentences to indicate 'A does not compare to B.' It is placed between the two noun phrases to be compared: A 没有 B... For example:

    1) 王丽莉没有陈凯文大。Lily Wang is not as old as Kevin Chen.

    2) 王丽莉家的人没有陈凯文家的人多。Lily Wang's family is not as large as Kevin Chen's.

    3) 学校里的菜没有家里的菜好吃。The food at school is not as good as the food at home.

4. 不 and 没 are the two most common negative particles in Mandarin Chinese. 不 is a general negation word whereas 没 is only used with 有. Sometimes, 有 may be omitted in 没有. For example:

    1) 我不认识她。I do not know her.

    2) 我的弟弟和妹妹不是大学生。My younger brother and sister are not college students.

    3) 我不爱吃学校的饭菜。I do not like to eat the food at school.

    4) 学生生活没(有)意思。Student life is not interesting.

    5) 中国学生没(有)美国学生多。There are not as many Chinese students as American students.

6) 我没(有)时间参加学生社团的活动。I do not have time to participate in student club activities.

Pattern Drill 1 句型操练一

Substitute the underlined parts in the following sentences with the expressions in the box.

1. A: 你去哪里？

   B: 我要去图书馆。

B. i. 上课
ii. 体育馆
iii. 吃午饭

2. 我每天除了上课，就是去图书馆。

i.	上课	自习
ii.	睡觉 (shuìjiào, sleep)	学习
iii.	学习	上网 (shàngwǎng, go online)

3. A: 你经常去图书馆吗？

   B: 是的，我经常去图书馆。

A. i.唱 KTV	B. i.唱 KTV
ii. 游泳	ii. 游泳
iii. 吃快餐	iii. 吃快餐

4. A: 你喜欢大学生活吗？

   B: 还好，就是太忙了。

A. i. 上大学 　　　　　 B. i. 功课太多了

ii. 打台球 　　　　　　　 ii. 不太会打

iii. 吃学校的饭菜 　　　　 iii. 太油 (yóu, greasy) 了

5. A: 什么时候<u>我请你去我家的餐馆吃饭</u>。

　 B: 好，一言为定。

A. i. 我介绍你参加一个中国学生社团

ii. 我们去体育馆打篮 (lán, basket) 球

iii. 我请你去看电影 (kàn diànyǐng, go to movies)

6. 我差点忘了<u>你家是开餐馆</u>。

i. 　　 你不是学数学的

ii. 　　 今天 (jīntiān, today)是你的生日(shēngrì, birthday)

iii. 　　 今天是星期天 (xīngqītiān，Sunday), 我不用(yòng, need) 上课

Pattern Drill 2 句型操练二

Unscramble the following sentences:

1. 去经图吗常书你馆？

2．欢学你饭喜吃校菜吗的？

3．你差餐忘了的开馆点我是。

4．候馆家请什去时饭我你餐吃么我的。

64

Pronunciation Drill 语音操练

Recite the classical poem 说日 with the help of *pinyin*, paying attention to the retroflex.

夏日无日日亦热，　　xià rì wú rì rì yì rè

冬日有日日亦寒，　　dōng rì yǒu rì rì yì hán

春日日出天渐暖，　　chūn rì rì chū tiān jiàn nuǎn

晒衣晒被晒褥单，　　sài yī sài bèi sài rù dān

秋日天高复云淡，　　qiū rì tiān gāo fù yún dàn

要看红日迫西山。　　yào kàn hóng rì pò xī shān

Exercises 练习

1. Write the Chinese characters that correspond to the following *pinyin*.

    1) sùshè   3) shètuán   5) cānjiā   7) yǒuyìsi

    2) liáotiān   4) tèbié   6) jīngcháng   8) shēnghuó

2. Match the words on the top line with words that typically go with them on the bottom line.

    上　　　　开　　　　参加　　　　交　　　　花　　　　学

    餐馆　　　　朋友　　　　东西　　　　钱　　　　课　　　　社团

3. Guess the meaning and sound of the following characters by breaking them down to their respective semantic and phonetic parts.

    1) 忠 = _____ + _____ sound: _____ meaning: _____

    2) 恨 = _____ + _____ sound: _____ meaning: _____

3) 腰 = _____ + _____ sound: _____ meaning: _____

4) 官 = _____ + _____ sound: _____ meaning: _____

5) 蓝 = _____ + _____ sound: _____ meaning: _____

4. Use each of the following characters to make two compound words and then write a sentence for each of the compound words.

1) 时 _____ _____

_____ _____

2) 习 _____ _____

_____ _____

3) 吃 _____ _____

_____ _____

4) 上 _____ _____

_____ _____

5. Fill in the blanks with the following words, using each word only once.

1) 没　　不

她_____经常去图书馆自习。

老师_____有学生多。

2) 不　　没

弹琴一点也_____有意思。

我一点也_____忙。

3) 除了...还　　　　除了...就是

学生生活很忙，每天_____上课，_____要自习。

学校生活没有意思，每天_____去教室，_____去图书馆。

4) 不过　还有

　　我很喜欢我的大学生活；_____，有时我也会想家。

　　学校的饭不好吃；_____，就是钱花得太快了。

6. Translate the following sentences into Chinese.

   1) She happens to be a college freshman, too.
   2) I almost forgot what your name is.
   3) There are not many Chinese student organizations on campus.
   4) In addition to studying, I also love to make friends.
   5) Except that money runs out too fast, I still like college life very much.
   6) College life is alright, but the food in the cafeteria is not as good as home-made food.

7. Correct mistakes in the following sentences.

   1) 我的学校没太大，不有体育馆。
   2) 学生活动中心除了有餐厅、商店，就是礼堂。
   3) 大学生活一点也不有意思。
   4) 每天除了上课，还是自习。
   5) A: 有时我请你去我家吃饭，好吗？
      B: 好的，我一定去。

8. Write a short paragraph (50 characters or more) about your student life. Please describe your daily routine, any student clubs you belong to, and how you like your campus life.

9. Research about student clubs on your campus. How many are there and what are they? Be prepared to share your findings with your classmates.

Character Stroke Order 生字笔画

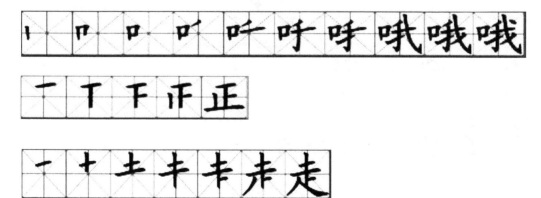

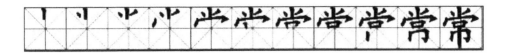

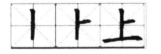

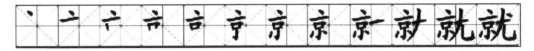

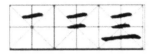

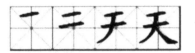

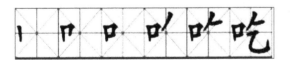

一 十 艹 艹 芏 芏 苹 苹 苹 菜

一 丁 丆 不

丶 冫 氵 氵 汐 汐 没

丶 丷 丷 芏 羊 羊 羊 差

丶 亠 亡 亡 忘 忘 忘

丶 讠 讠 订 请 请 请 请 请

丶 丶 忄 忄 忙 忙

刁 习 习

ㄥ ㄙ 厽 厽 矣 矣 参 参

乛 力 加 加 加

丶 ㇇ 礻 礻 社 社 社

丨 冂 月 用 用 用

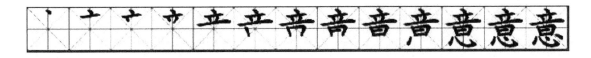

丶 一 十 六 立 产 产 音 音 音 意 意 意

丿 口 日 甲 田 田 思 思 思

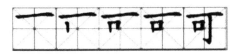

一 ナ 大 太

丶 亠 亠 亠 立 立 辛 亲 亲 亲 新 新 新

一 丁 可 口 可

丶 亠 六 六 夯 交

丿 刀 月 月 刖 朋 朋 朋

一 ナ 方 友

一 丆 丌 丌 耳 耳 耴 耴 耴 聊 聊

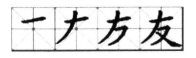

一 寸 寸 寸 讨 过

丿 ヒ 牛 牛 牜 牜 特 特 特 特

丶 口 口 号 另 別 别

70

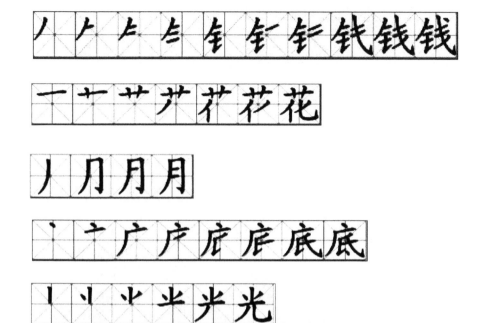

丿 𠂆 𠂉 𠂢 钅 钅 钅 钱 钱 钱

一 十 艹 艹 艹 花 花

丿 刀 月 月

丶 亠 广 庐 庐 庐 底 底

丨 丬 业 业 半 光 光

Unit Three 第三单元

My Community 我的社区

Lesson 5 第五课 My Neighborhood 我的街区

Think and Share 想想说说

1. 你家住在哪里？Where does your family live?
2. 你家附近有中国店吗？Are there any Chinese stores near your home?
3. 你的街区交通方便吗？Is transportation convenient in your neighborhood?
4. 你喜欢你的街区吗？为什么？How do you like your neighborhood? Why?

Dialogue 对话

陈凯文：丽莉，你家住在哪里？

王丽莉：我家住在皇后区七十五大道八十八街。

陈凯文：你家附近有中国店吗？

王丽莉：当然有。有超市，餐馆，洗衣店，理发店，还有 KTV 呢。

陈凯文：你的街区交通方便吗？

王丽莉：还可以，有巴士，也有地铁。不过，从我家到地铁站要走二十分钟的路。

陈凯文：你的街区停车方便吗？

王丽莉：不太方便，虽然有停车场，但是总是停得满满的，停车费也蛮贵的。

陈凯文：那你们上街是走路，坐车，还是自己开车呢？

王丽莉：不一定，近的就走路，远的就坐车，去超市一般都会开车。

陈凯文：你喜欢你的街区吗？

王丽莉：还好吧。虽然交通不太方便，但是蛮安静的，也比较安全。

陈凯文：什么时候我去你的街区看看，欢迎吗？

王丽莉：当然，欢迎你有时间来我家做客。

Answer Questions 回答问题

1. 王丽莉的家住在哪里？Where is Lily Wang's home located?
2. 她家附近有中国店吗？Are there any Chinese stores near her home?
3. 她的街区交通方便吗？Is transportation convenient in her neighborhood?
4. 她喜不喜欢她的街区？为什么？Does she like her neighborhood? Why?

Vocabulary 生词

1. 社区	shèqū	n	community
2. 街区	jiēqū	n	neighborhood; block
3. 区	qū	n	district; borough
4. 大道	dàdào	n	avenue
5. 街	jiē	n	street
6. 店	diàn	n	store
7. 附近	fùjìn	n	nearby
8. 当然	dāngrán	adv	of course
9. 超市	chāoshì	n	supermarket
10. 洗衣店	xǐyīdiàn	n	laundromat
11. 理发店	lǐfàdiàn	n	barber shop
12. 交通	jiāotōng	n	traffic; transportation
13. 方便	fāngbiàn	adj/n	convenient; convenience
14. 巴士	bāshì	n	bus
15. 地铁	dìtiě	n	subway
16. 站	zhàn	v/n	to stand ; stop
17. 分钟	fēnzhōng	n	minute
18. 路	lù	n	road; way
19. 停车	tíngchē	v/n	to stop a car; to park; parking
20. 虽然	suīrán	conj	although
21. 停车场	tíngchēchǎng	n	parking lot; parking garage
22. 但是	dànshì	conj	but

74

23. 总是	zǒngshì	adv	always
24. 满	mǎn	adj	full
25. 费	fèi	n	fee
26. 蛮	mán	adv	(collq) quite; rather
27. 贵	guì	adj	expensive
28. 上街	shàngjiē	v	to go shopping
29. 走路	zǒulù	v	to walk
30. 坐	zuò	v	to sit
31. 坐车	zuòchē	v	to ride in a car, bus, or subway
32. 开车	kāichē	v	to drive
33. 不一定	bùyīdìng	idiom	It depends ; not necessarily
34. 近	jìn	adj	near; close
35. 远	yuǎn	adj	far
36. 一般	yìbān	adv	generally
37. 安静	ānjìng	adj	quiet
38. 比较	bǐjiào	adv	rather; relatively
39. 安全	ānquán	adj	safe
40. 看	kàn	v	to look
41. 欢迎	huānyíng	v/n	to welcome; welcome
42. 时间	shíjiān	n	time
43. 做客	zuòkè	v	to be a guest

Proper Nouns 专有名词

| 1．皇后区 | huánghòuqū | Queens Borough |

75

Short Reading 阅读短文

　　我家住在市郊，离市区开车要半个小时。每个周末我们全家都会开车去城里买东西、去餐馆吃饭。我的街区有商店，餐馆，还有学校，医院，和公园。虽然交通不太方便，但是比较安静，也比较安全。我很喜欢我的街区，因为到处都是绿草坪，很美，邻居也很友好。

Answer Questions 回答问题

1．作者的家离市区有多远？How far is the writer's home away from the city proper?
2．他们家多长时间去一次城里？How often does his/her family go to the city?
3．他们家去城里做什么？ What does his/her family do in the city?
4．他/她的街区都有些什么？ What does his/her neighborhood have?
5．他/她的街区怎么样？How is his/her neighborhood?
6．作者喜欢他/她的街区吗？为什么？How doesthe writer like his/her neighborhood? Why？

Vocabulary 生词

1. 市郊	shìjiāo	n	suburb
2. 离	lí	prep	away from
3. 市区	shìqū	n	city proper
4. 半	bàn	adj	half
5. 小时	xiǎoshí	n	hour
6. 周末	zhōumò	n	weekend
7. 全	quán	a	all of; complete
8. 城里	chéngli	n	inner city
9. 买	mǎi	v	to buy; to shop
10. 医院	yīyuàn	n	hospital
11. 公园	gōngyuán	n	park
12. 邻居	línjū	n	neighbor
13. 友好	yǒuhǎo	adj	friendly

Task 1 Individual Work 个人活动

Draw a map of your neighborhood and label streets as well as important landmarks such as stores, restaurants, schools, subway and/or bus stations, parks (公园), post office (邮局), banks (银行), fire stations (消防站) and etc.

Task 2 Pair Activity 双人活动

With a partner, role-play the following situation in 4 to 5 sentences each. Your friend invites you to his/her house or a place in his/her neighborhood. You ask him/her for directions. On your way there, you are lost. Call your friend for further directions. Use the map your partner has drawn as a aid if necessary. You may optionally perform this skit to the whole class.

Character Notes 汉字讲解

1. 右耳刀

   The 'right ear knigh' on the right side of the character implies 'town' or 'city.'
   For example:

郊	jiāo	n	suburb
邻	lín	n	neighbor
那	nà	pron/conj	that; in that case
都	dū/dōu	n/adv	capital city; all

2. 左耳刀

   The 'left ear knigh' implies 'mound' or 'steepness.' For example:

院	yuàn	n	yard
附	fù	v	to be close to; be attached to
除	chú	prep/v	except; to remove

3. 金字旁

   The 'gold radical' implies 'gold' or 'metal.' For example:

钟	zhōng	n	clock
铁	tiě	n	iron
钱	qián	n	money

4. 玉字旁

The 'jade radical' implies 'treasure.' For example:

理	lǐ	n/v	reason; to manage
球	qiú	n	ball
玩	wán	v	to play

Grammar and Usage 语法讲解

1. 从我家到地铁站要走二十分钟的路 means 'From my home to the subway station takes 20 minutes on foot.' Another way to say it is 从我家到地铁站走路要二十分钟 'From my home to the subway station by foot takes 20 minutes.' They are mutually exchangeable. For example:
   1) 从学校到城里要开一个小时的车。From the school to the city takes one hour by car.
   2) 从学校到城里开车要一个小时。From the school to the city by car takes one hour.
   2) 我们在城里要买一天的东西。We are going to do one day of shopping in the city.
   4) 我们在城里买东西要一天(的时间)。It takes one day's time for us to shop in the city.

2. 虽然...但是... is a common sentence pattern meaning 'although...but...'. Unlike in English, 但是 (but) is obligatory, not redundant. For example:
   1) 虽然大学生活很有意思，但是我有时还会想家。Although college life is interesting, (but) I still miss home occasionally.
   2) 虽然我是从中国来的，但是我的中文说得不太好。Although I came from China, my Chinese is not so good.

3. 满满 'full' and 看看 'to take a look' are examples of reduplication that is commonly found in Mandarin Chinese. When adjectives and adverbs are reduplicated, they become more descriptive and stronger in degree. When verbs are reduplicated, they mean to do something for a little while. The second syllable in a reduplicated word usually takes a neutral tone. For example:
   1) 你要好好学习。You must study really hard.
   2) 我想快快毕业、早早工作。I want to graduate really fast and start working really soon.
   3) 我们来聊聊天。Let's chat for a while.

4) 每个周末我和家人都会去中国城吃吃饭、买买东西。Every weekend me and my family would go to Chinatown to eat and shop for a little while.

4. 是...还是... 'or' introduces two or more options in an interrogative sentence. Before a verb phrase, 是 is often omitted. For example:
   1) 你是中国人还是美国人？Are you Chinese or American?
   2) 他是大学生还是中学生？Is he a college student or high school student?
   3) 你(是)喜欢音乐还是体育？Do you like music or physical education?
   4) 她(是)坐车还是走路来的？Did she come by car or by foot?

5. 近的就走路，远的就开车 'If it is close, (I) will walk; if it is far, (I) will drive.' In this sentence, adj + 的 makes a noun out of an adjective meaning 'the one that is ...' For example:
   1) 你有好吃的吗？Do you have anything that's good to eat?
   2) 你要贵的还是便宜的？Do you want the expensive one or the cheap one?
   3) 我要一个新的。I want a new one.

Pattern Drill 1 句型操练一

Substitute the underlined parts in the following sentences with phrases in the box.

1. A: 你家住在哪里？

   B: 我家住在皇后区七十五大道八十八街。

   > B. i. 纽约 (niǔyuē, New York)
   >
   > ii. 中国北京
   >
   > iii. 加州 (jiāzhōu, California)

2. A: 你家附近有中国店吗？

   B: 有超市，餐馆，洗衣店，理发店，还有 KTV 呢。

79

A. i. 你的社区 大学	B. i. 大学、地铁站、书店 超市
ii. 你宿舍前边 楼房	ii. 体育馆、学生中心 图书馆
iii. 你学校附近 超市	iii. 有超市、电影院 火车站

3．从我家到地铁站要走二十分钟的路.

A. i. 大学	B. i. 我家
ii. 纽约大学	ii. 中国城
iii. 宿舍	iii. 体育馆

4. 那你们是走路，坐车，还是自己开车呢？

i.	中国人，日本人，韩国人
ii.	去上课，打篮球，去游泳
iii.	吃美国菜，中国菜，法国 (fǎguó, French)菜

5. 虽然交通不太方便，但是比较安静。

A. i. 数学很难 (nán, hard)	B. i. 很有用 (yǒuyòng, useful)
ii. 电影很长	ii. 蛮有意思的
iii. 中文功课很多	iii. 考试 (kǎoshì, test) 很容易(róngyì, easy)

Pattern Drill 2 句型操练二

Unscramble the following sentences:

1. 国附家店近中你吗有？

2. 在哪住里家你？

3. 路们是街走上你，车开是己呢还自？

4. 便通然交不虽方太，的蛮是静但安。

5. 家欢我客有间你做时迎来。

Exercises 练习

1. Write the Chinese characters that correspond to the following words in *pinyin*.

   1) jiēqū   3) fùjìn   5) jiāotōng   7) fāngbiàn

   2) huānyíng   4) zuòkè   6) lí   8) línjū

2. Match the words on the top lines with words that typically go with them on the bottom line.

   交通   买   上   坐   走   做

   路   车   客   东西   方便   街

3. Guess the meaning and sound of the following characters by breaking them down to their respective semantic and phonetic parts.

   1) 邮 = _____ + _____ sound: _____ meaning: _____

   2) 阶 = _____ + _____ sound: _____ meaning: _____

81

3) 铜 = ＿＿＿ + ＿＿＿ sound: ＿＿＿ meaning: ＿＿＿＿＿

4) 现 = ＿＿＿ + ＿＿＿ sound: ＿＿＿ meaning: ＿＿＿＿＿

4. Use the following Chinese characters to form two compound words and make a sentence for each of the compound words.

　1) 区　　　＿＿＿＿＿　　　＿＿＿＿＿＿＿＿＿＿＿＿＿＿

　　　　　　＿＿＿＿＿　　　＿＿＿＿＿＿＿＿＿＿＿＿＿＿

　2) 车　　　＿＿＿＿＿　　　＿＿＿＿＿＿＿＿＿＿＿＿＿＿

　　　　　　＿＿＿＿＿　　　＿＿＿＿＿＿＿＿＿＿＿＿＿＿

　3) 安　　　＿＿＿＿＿　　　＿＿＿＿＿＿＿＿＿＿＿＿＿＿

　　　　　　＿＿＿＿＿　　　＿＿＿＿＿＿＿＿＿＿＿＿＿＿

　4) 市　　　＿＿＿＿＿　　　＿＿＿＿＿＿＿＿＿＿＿＿＿＿

　　　　　　＿＿＿＿＿　　　＿＿＿＿＿＿＿＿＿＿＿＿＿＿

5. Fill in the blanks with the words given, using each word only once.

　1) 当然　一定

　　A: 你的社区有游泳池吗？

　　B: ＿＿＿＿＿有，就在公园里。

　2) A: 有时间我们一起去游泳，好吗？

　　B: 好的，我＿＿＿＿＿去。

　3) 虽然...但是... 是...还是...

　　我们上街＿＿＿＿＿吃饭＿＿＿＿＿买东西？

　　这个超市的东西＿＿＿＿＿很多，＿＿＿＿＿比较贵。

　4) 从　　　离

　　我家＿＿＿＿＿中国城很近，走路只要十分钟就到了。

　　＿＿＿＿＿我家走路到中国城只要十分钟。

82

5) 要　　会

A: 请你一定__________来我家做客呀。

B: 好，有时间我一定 __________去的。

6. Translate the following sentences into Chinese.

1) My family lives on 6th Avenue and 143 Street in Queens.
2) It takes 30 minutes to walk from my home to the subway station.
3) Although transportation is inconvenient in my neighborhood, it is pretty quiet.
4) I walk to the stores nearby and take the bus to the ones far away.
5) Do you like to live in the city or the suburb?
6) It depends. Life in the city is relatively convenient, but the suburb is relatively safe.
7) I don't like the parking in the city. The parking garage is often full and expensive.
8) You are welcome to visit my home when you have the time.

7. Correct mistakes in the following sentences.

1) 我家没有中国店在附近。
2) 从我家到市区要开车一个小时。
3) 我家一般都每个周末会去城里买东西。
4) 中国城虽然很远，可以那里买到很多好吃的东西。
5) 城里的停车很不方便和很贵。
6) 我的街区都有中国店和餐馆，不过东西比较贵和不好吃。

8. Write a short paragraph (50 or more characters) about your neighborhood. Say where it is located, what is in it and if it is convenient. State if you like your neighborhood or not and why.

Character Stroke Order 生字笔画

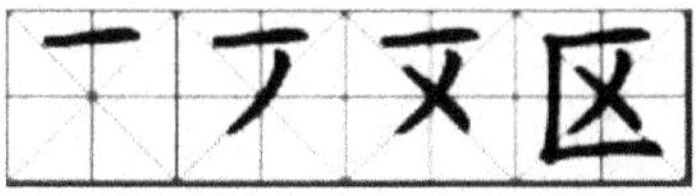

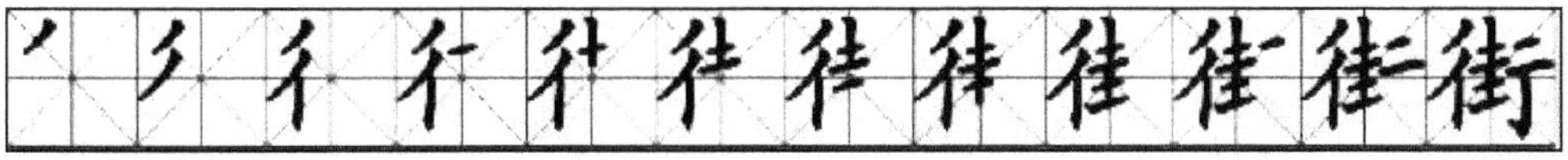

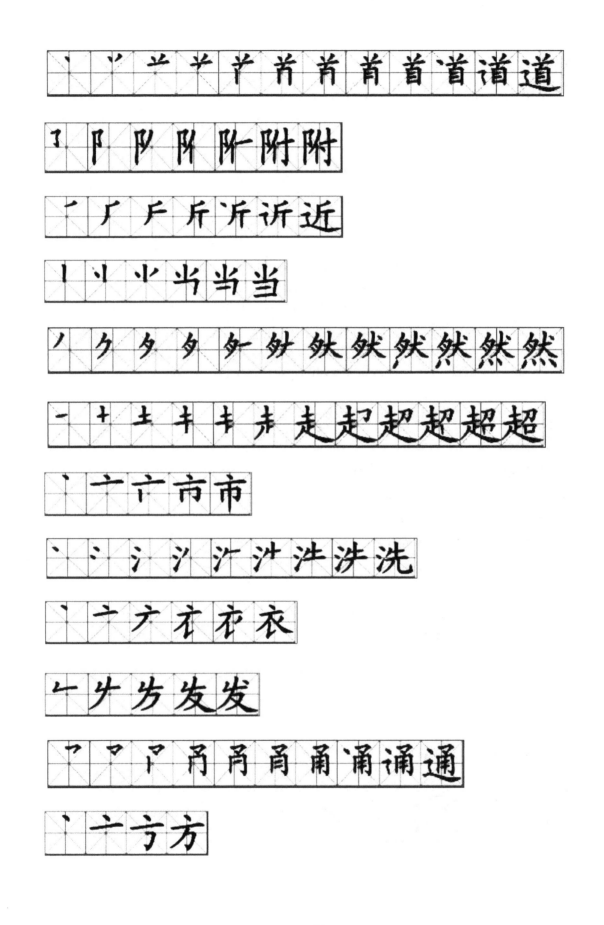

84

全　丿 人 仐 仐 仐 全

看　一 二 三 丢 丢 看 看 看 看

迎　丿 亻 幻 印 印 迎 迎

间　丶 门 门 门 问 问 间

客　丶 宀 宀 宀 岁 安 安 客 客

郊　丶 亠 六 六 交 交 郊 郊

离　丶 一 亠 文 这 卤 卤 离 离 离

半　丶 丷 丷 半 半

周　丿 几 月 用 用 用 周 周

末　一 二 丰 才 末

买　丁 乛 乛 买 买 买

院　乛 阝 阝 阝 阡 陀 陀 陀 院

87

丁 ㄱ 尸 尸 尺 居 居 居

88

Lesson 6 第六课 Chinatown 中国城

Think and Share 想想说说

1. 你有没有去过中国城？Have you been to Chinatown before?
2. 你去中国城都做些什么？What do you do in Chinatown?
3. 你喜不喜欢中国城？为什么？Do you like Chinatown? Why?

Dialogue 对话

王丽莉：凯文，你家住在哪里？

陈凯文：我家就住在中国城里，离我家开的餐馆不远。

王丽莉：你家的餐馆在哪条街上？

陈凯文：在勿街跟百老汇的交叉路口上。

王丽莉：那你家在哪条街上呢？

陈凯文：我家住在孔子大厦里。

王丽莉：你家为什么要住在中国城里呢？

陈凯文：因为生活方便呀。到处都是商店、餐馆，上班只要走过几个路口就到了。

王丽莉：去中国城有地铁吗？

陈凯文：当然有，四号或者六号地铁都去中国城，到坚尼街站下车就到了。

王丽莉：除了回家和上班以外，你都喜欢到中国城的哪里玩？

陈凯文：我最喜欢去坚尼街打台球，或者去百老汇唱 KTV.

王丽莉：什么时候我跟你去勿街唱 KTV，好吗？

陈凯文：没问题，一言为定。

Answer Questions 回答问题

1. 陈凯文的家住在中国城的哪里？Where in Chinatown is Kevin Chen's home located?
2. 他家为什么住在中国城里？Why does his family live in Chinatown?

3. 他家的餐馆在哪条街上？On which street is his family restaurant located?

4. 去中国城有没有地铁？Are there any subway lines that go to Chinatown?

5. 几号地铁去中国城？Which subway lines go to Chinatown?

6. 在哪个站下车可以到中国城？Which stop does one get off to go to Chinatown?

Vocabulary 生词

1. 哪	nǎ	pron	which
2. 条	tiáo	m	(measure word for street , road, river, pants)
3. 交叉	jiāochā	n/adj	cross; crossed
4. 路口	lùkǒu	n	intersection; block
5. 上	shàng	prep	on
6. 大厦	dàshà	n	high building
7. 上班	shàngbān	v	to go to work
8. 过	guò	v/part	to pass; (experiential particle)
9. 号	hào	n	number
10. 下车	xiàchē	v	to get off
11. 最	zuì	adv	most
12. 或者	huòzhě	conj	or
13. 问题	wèntí	n	question; problem

Proper Nouns 专有名词

1. 勿街	wùjiē	Mott Street
2. 百老汇	bǎilǎohuì	Broadway
3. 孔子	kǒngzǐ	Confucius
4. 坚尼街	jiānníjiē	Canal Street

Short Reading 阅读短文

我家住在中国城，离市中心很近。中国城从早到晚都很热闹，到处都是商店、中餐馆、菜市场，还有医院、学校、教堂、和街心公园。中国城虽然比较吵闹，但是生活方便，去哪里都可以走得到，还有很多地铁和巴士，可以坐到市区的每一个街区。中国城里住着很多从中国来的新移民，主要是广东人和福建人，也有其他国家的华裔移民。

Answer Questions 回答问题

1. 中国城离市中心远吗？Is Chinatown far from the city center?
2. 中国城都有些什么？What are there in Chinatown?
3. 中国城的交通方便吗？为什么？Is transportation convenient in Chinatown? Why?
4. 住在中国城里的主要是什么人？Who are the primary residents in Chinatown?

Vocabulary 生词

1.	市中心	shìzhōngxīn	n	city center; downtown
2.	早	zǎo	adj/n	early; morning
3.	晚	wǎn	adj/n	late; evening
4.	热闹	rènao	adj	bustling with noise and excitement
5.	菜市场	càishìchǎng	n	vegetable stands; farmer's market
6.	教堂	jiàotáng	n	church
7.	街心	jiēxīn	n	street corner
8.	吵闹	chǎonào	adj	noisy
9.	着	zhe	part	(to indicate continuous or stationary status)
10.	主要	zhǔyào	adj/adv	main; mainly
11.	其他	qítā	adj	other
12.	国家	guójiā	n	country; nation
13.	华裔	huáyì	adj	of Chinese descent

Proper Nouns 专有名词

1. 福建   fújiàn   Fujian

Task 1 Pair Activity 双人活动

Role-play a tourist lost in Chinatown. Try to ask a passerby for directions to your destination. You may want to look at a map of Chinatown.

Task 2 Group/Class Activity 小组/课堂活动

Role-play the following situation. An amount of money has been made available to address an urgent issue facing Chinatown. You are respectively a group of residents, business owners, customers, police, sanitation workers, etc. of Chinatown. Deliver a mini persuasive speech at a townhall meeting in which you argue for how the money should be spent. Only one group will be rewarded the money by popular vote at the end of the meeting. Each member of a group should assume a part of the speech.

Characters Notes 汉字讲解

1. 方框

   The 'frame radical' implies 'enclosure.' For example:

国	guó	n	country; nation
园	gyuán	n	garden
团	tuán	n	group
图	tú	n	picture

2. 门字框

   The 'door radical' implies 'door.' For example:

问	wèn	v	ro ask
闹	nào	adj	noisy
间	jiān	n/m	room; (measure word for room)

3. 走字旁

   The 'walk radical" implies 'walking' or 'running.' For example:

走	zǒu	v	to walk
超	chāo	v/adj	to pass; super
起	qǐ	v	to rise

92

4. 足字旁

The 'foot radical' implies 'foot.' For example:

路	lù	n	road
跟	gēn	v/prep	to follow; with

Grammar and Usage 语法讲解

1. In Chinese, 的 is commonly used before a noun phrase to introduce a modifier. Here are some examples of various types of nominal modifiers introduced by 的:

   1) Pron/N + 的 to indicate possessive
      我的家 'my family'
      你的名字 'your name'
      他的朋友 'his friend'
      市区的每一个街区 'every neighborhood in the city'
   2) Adj + 的 to describe the attribute of the noun phrase
      热闹的商店 'busy store'
      方便的交通 'convenient transportation'
      绿绿的草坪 'really green lawn'
      新的东西 'new things'
   3) Relative Clause + 的 to restrict the reference of the noun phrase
      我家开的餐馆 'the restaurant owned by my family'
      从中国来的新移民 'the new immigrants that come from China'

2. 最 'most' is a superlative marker which is placed before an adjective, adverb, or a verb to describe the highest degree. For example:
   1) 最吵闹的街区 'the noisiest neighborhood'
   2) 最早来美国的移民 'the earliest immigrant to America'
   3) 我最喜欢的东西 'my favorite thing'

3. In Chinese, there are different words that correspond to the English word 'or' depending on the sentence type: affirmative sentence, negative sentence, or interrogative sentence. For example:
   1) Affirmative sentence 或者
      我们打篮球或者唱KTV。 We play basketball or sing karaoke.
      你可以选数学或者化学。 You can choose either math or chemistry.

2) Negative sentence 也不/也没

我不会弹钢琴，也不会唱歌。I don't know how to play the piano or sing.

我没有弟弟，也没有妹妹。I don't have a younger brother or a younger sister.

3) Interrogative sentence 还是

你喜欢吃中国餐还是美国餐？Do you like Chinese food or American food?

你是去上班还是去上学？Are you going to work or going to school?

Cultural information 文化常识

孔子 Confucius (551BC-476BC) is a famous Chinese philosopher born in the late Spring-Autumn Period. His teachings about social morality and personal virtues can be found in the <u>Analects of Confucius</u> and have had a profound influence on the thoughts and lives of Chinese, Korean, Japanese and Vietnamese societies for the past 2000 years.

Pattern Drill 句型操练

Substitute the underlined parts in the following sentences with the expressions in the box.

1. <u>我家</u>离<u>我家开的餐馆</u><u>不远</u>。

i. 宿舍	行政楼	很近
ii. 中国城	市中心	不远
iii. 纽约	北京	很远

2. A: 你为什么要<u>住在中国城里</u>呢？

    B: 因为<u>生活方便呀</u>。

A. i. 去中国城	B. i. 可以吃中国菜呀
ii. 搬(bān, move)出去	ii. 宿舍太小了
iii. 到外州(wài zhōu, out of state)去念大学呢	iii. 这里没有我要念的专业

3. A: 除了回家或者上班以外，你都喜欢到中国城的哪里玩？

B: 我最喜欢去坚尼街打台球，或者勿街唱 KTV。

A. i. 英文和中文　　还会说什么语言(yǔyán, language)?

B. i. 我还会说日文(rìwén, Japanese)

A. ii. 中餐和西餐　　还喜欢吃什么餐？

B. ii. 我还喜欢吃法国餐。

A. iii. 弹钢琴和唱歌　　还喜欢做什么？

B. iii. 去体育馆打球　去游泳池 (chí, pool) 游泳。

Pronunciation Drill 语音操练

Practice the following saying by Confucius with the help of *pinyin,* paying attention to the retroflex initial *zh* and the final *i.*

知之为知之，　　　　zhī zhī wéi zhī zhī

不知为不知，　　　　bù zhī wéi bù zhī

不以不知为知之，　　bù yǐ bù zhī wéi zhī zhī

不以知之为不知，　　bù yǐ zhī zhī wéi bù zhī

唯此才能求真知。　　wéi cǐ cái néng qiú zhēn zhī

Exercises 练习

1.　Write the Chinese characters that correspond to the following *pinyin.*

1) dàshà　　　3) jiēkǒu　　　5) huòzhě　　　7) wèntí

2) chǎonào　　4) guójiā　　　6) huáyì　　　8) rènao

2. Match the words on the top line with words that typically go with them on the bottom line.

回　　　　住在　　　　住着　　　　生活　　　　交叉　　　　从早

方便　　　移民　　　　路口　　　　家　　　　到晚　　　　城里

3. Guess the meaning and sound of the following characters by breaking them down to their respective semantic and phonetic parts.

1) 回 = _____ + _____ sound: _____ meaning: _____

2) 闷 = _____ + _____ sound: _____ meaning: _____

3) 赶 = _____ + _____ sound: _____ meaning: _____

4) 跑 = _____ + _____ sound: _____ meaning: _____

4. Use the following Chinese characters to form two compound words and make a sentence for each of the compound words.

1) 口　_____　_____

　　　　 _____　_____

2) 下　_____　_____

　　　　 _____　_____

3) 路　_____　_____

　　　　 _____　_____

4) 心　_____　_____

　　　　 _____　_____

5. Fill in the blanks with the words given.

1) 或者　　　　还是　　　　也不

A: 你喜欢住在城里_____住在市郊？

B: 我不喜欢住在城里，_____喜欢住在市郊。

A: 可是，你一定要住在城里，_____住在市郊。

2) 的　　　　　得

城里_____停车场，车总是停_____满满的。

我们去_____中国城，从早到晚都很热闹。

中国城_____生活很方便，哪里都可以走_____到。

3) 最　　　　　都

坐地铁或者巴士，_____可以到中国城。

在学校里，我_____想吃家里的饭菜。

6. Translate the following sentences into Chinese.

1) My family lives in a neighborhood not far from Chinatown.
2) From my home to Chinatown takes only 10 minutes by foot.
3) Although Chinatown is relatively noisy, (but) life is rather convenient.
4) There are many Chinese restaurants, stores, food markets in Chinatown.
5) Many new immigrants from China live in Chinatown.

7. Correct the mistakes in the following sentences.

1) 我家住在一个街区离市中心很近的。
2) 从我家到市中心只要走几个街口到了。
3) 市中心得交通很方便，去哪里都走的到。
4) 住在市区虽然很方便，太吵闹了。
5) 中国城里住着很多从广东还是福建来的新移民。

8. Write a short paragraph (50 or more characters) about your favorite place in Chinatown. Please specify what type of establishment it is, its location, what the place has to offer, and why it is your favorite place.

9. Research about a major Chinatown in the U.S. Find out about its location, origin, population, amenities it offers as well as its problems. Share your with your class.

Character Stroke Order 生字笔画

丶 厂 厂 厂 厍 厍 厍 厍 厍 厦 厦

丶 冂 冃 日 旦 旱 昂 昂 昌 最 最

一 厂 厅 可 可 或 或 或

一 十 土 耂 耂 老 者 者

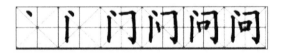

一 十 扌 执 执 执 热 热 热

丶 冂 门 门 闩 闹 闹 闹

98

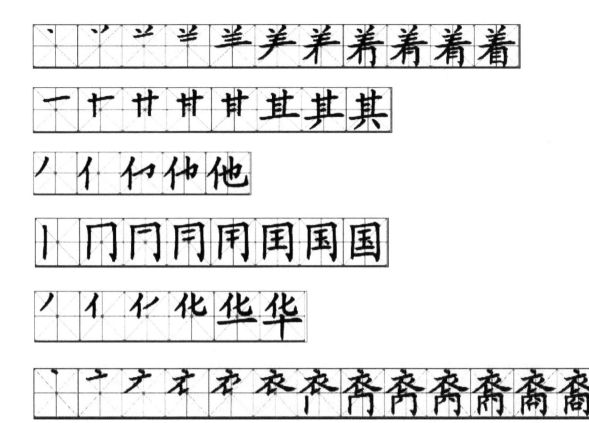

、 ゛ 丷 丷 羊 差 差 着 着 着

一 十 卅 卅 甘 其 其 其

丿 亻 仈 仳 他

丨 冂 冂 同 用 囯 国 国

丿 亻 仕 化 华 华

、 宀 广 亢 充 衣 衣 产 产 产 斋 斋 斋

Unit Four 第四单元

My Social Life 我的社交活动

Source:Tupian.baike.com

Lesson 7 第七课 Eating out at a Chinese Restaurant 在中餐馆吃饭

Think and Share 想想说说

1. 你有没有去过中餐馆喝早茶？Have you had morning tea in a Chinese restaurant?
2. 喝茶有什么讲究？What are some of the customs involved in tea drinking?
3. 你最喜欢吃哪些点心？What are your favorite 'dim sum'?
4. 中国有哪几大菜系？What are the major branches of regional Chinese cuisine?

Dialogue 对话

陈凯文：丽莉，我们到了，这就是我家开的中餐馆。

王丽莉：哇，这么大的餐馆，生意一定很兴隆吧。

陈凯文：还可以吧。请进。

服务员：欢迎光临。请问, 几位？

陈凯文：两位。

服务员：请跟我来。请坐。两位要喝什么茶？

王丽莉：我喜欢喝珍珠奶茶。

服务员：对不起，我们没有珍珠奶茶。

陈凯文：那就来两杯绿茶，一碟凤爪和一碟小菜吧。

服务员：好的，两杯绿茶，一碟凤爪和一碟小菜。这是你们的菜单。

陈凯文：丽莉，你来点菜，我请客。

王丽莉：那我就不客气了。我想尝尝你们的清蒸龙利。

陈凯文：好，一个清蒸龙利，一个葱爆龙虾。

服务员：这是你们点的清蒸龙利、葱爆龙虾。请慢用。

王丽莉：这个清蒸龙利真好吃。

陈凯文：是呀，这是我们家的拿手菜。你也尝尝我点的葱爆龙虾吧。

王丽莉：那个葱爆龙虾也很好吃。

陈凯文：什么时候我炒几个菜让你尝尝。

王丽莉：那好呀，我真有口福。

陈凯文：服务员，买单。

王丽莉：凯文，谢谢你请我吃饭。下次请你到我家做客。

Answer Questions 回答问题

1. 王丽莉和陈凯文去哪家中餐馆吃饭？Which Chinese restaurant did Lily Wang and Kevin Chen go to?
2. 是谁请客？Who was paying for the meal?
3. 王丽莉点了什么菜？What did Lily Wang oder?
4. 陈凯文点了什么菜？What did Kevin Chen order?
5. 这家中餐馆的拿手菜是什么？What is the house special in this restaurant?
6. 陈凯文家的餐馆是属于哪个菜系呢？Which regional cuisine does Kevin's family restaurant specialize in?

Vocabulary 生词

1.	哇	wa	int	wow
2.	生意	shēngyì	n	business
3.	兴隆	xīnglóng	adj	brisk (business); prosperous
4.	进	jìn	v	to enter
5.	服务员	fúwùyuán	n	waiter; waitress
6.	欢迎光临	huānyíngguānglín	idiom	welcome (formal)
7.	问	wèn	v	to ask
8.	位	wèi	n/m	seat; (measure word for people)
9.	两	liǎng	nu	two (used before measure word)
10.	喝	hē	v	to drink
11.	茶	chá	n	tea
12.	奶	nǎi	n	milk

13. 对不起	duìbuqǐ	idiom	sorry; excuse me
14. 杯	bēi	n/m	cup; (measure for liquid)
15. 碟	dié	n/m	plate; (measure word for dish)
16. 小菜	xiǎocài	n	pickles
17. 菜单	càidān	n	menu
18. 点	diǎn	v	to order (food)
19. 请客	qǐngkè	v	to treat someone
20. 客气	kèqi	adj	polite
21. 尝	cháng	v	to taste
22. 慢用	mànyòng	idiom	bon appetite
23. 真	zhēn	adv	really
24. 拿手菜	náshǒucài	n	special dish
25. 炒	chǎo	v	to stir-fry
26. 让	ràng	v	to let
27. 口福	kǒufú	n	gastronomic luck
28. 买单	mǎidān	v	to pay the bill
29. 谢谢	xiè xiè	idiom	thanks
30. 下次	xiàcì	adv	next time
31. 次	*cì*	m	(measure word for 'time')

Proper Nouns 专有名词

1.珍珠奶茶	zhēnzhū nǎichá	pearl milk tea; bubble tea
3.凤爪	fèngzhuǎ	chicken claw
4.清蒸龙利	qīngzhēnglónglì	steamed founder

103

5. 葱爆龙虾	cōngbàolóngxiā	stir-fried lobster with scallion

Short Reading 阅读短文

　　每个星期天上午，我们全家都会去中国城喝早茶。喝茶的人很多，所有的桌子都坐满了人，还有不少人站着排队。早茶的品种很多，有绿茶、红茶、还有花茶。点心的品种也是五花八门，有叉烧包、莲蓉包、烧卖、虾饺等等，还有各式各样的小炒。我最喜欢吃芝麻球、皮蛋粥、和肠粉。我们全家一边品尝早茶，一边聊天，非常开心。

Answer Questions 回答问题

1. 作者全家什么时候去中国城喝早茶？When does the writer's family go to Chinatown for morning tea?
2. 为什么说喝茶的人很多？Why is it said that there are many people there for morning tea?
3. 早茶都有哪些品种？What types of tea are there?
4. 点心都有哪些品种？What types of dim sum are there?
5. 作者最喜欢吃什么点心？What are the writer's favorite dim sum?
6. 作者全家一边喝早茶，一边做什么？What does the writer's family do when they are having morning tea?

Vocabulary 生词

1. 星期	xīngqī	n	week
2. 星期天	xīngqītiān	n	Sunday
3. 上午	shàngwǔ	n	morning
4. 早茶	zǎochá	n	morning tea
5. 所有	suóyǒu	adj	all
6. 桌子	zhuōzi	n	table
7. 不少	bùshǎo	adj	quite a few
8. 排队	páiduì	v	to stand in line; to queue up
9. 品种	pǐnzhǒng	n	variety
10. 红	hóng	adj	red

11. 点心	diǎnxin	n	dumplings; dim sum
12. 五花八门	wǔhuābāmén	idiom	multivarious; of a wide variety
13. 各式各样	gèshìgèyàng	idiom	all kinds of
14. 小炒	xiǎochǎo	n	small stir-fried dish
15. 一边	yìbiān	adv	at the same time
16. 品尝	pǐncháng	v	to taste; to savor

Proper Nouns 专有名词

1·叉烧包	chāshāobāo	steamed bun with Chinese barbeque pork
2·莲蓉包	liánróngbāo	steamed bun with sweet lotus seed paste
3·烧卖	shāomai	steamed dumpling with minced pork
4·虾饺	xiājiǎo	steamed dumpling with shrimp
5·芝麻球	zhīmáqiú	deep-fried sesame ball with sweet bean paste
6·皮蛋粥	pídànzhōu	egg congee
7·肠粉	chángfěn	soft rice noodle

Task 1 Group Activity 小组活动

In a group of three or four, role-play dining out in a Chinese restaurant with your friend(s). Please Use a real menu from a Chinese restaurant to order food.

Task 2 Class Activity 全班活动

Pick a favorite Chinese dish of your family and tell your classmates why it is your favorite dish and how to prepare it step by step.

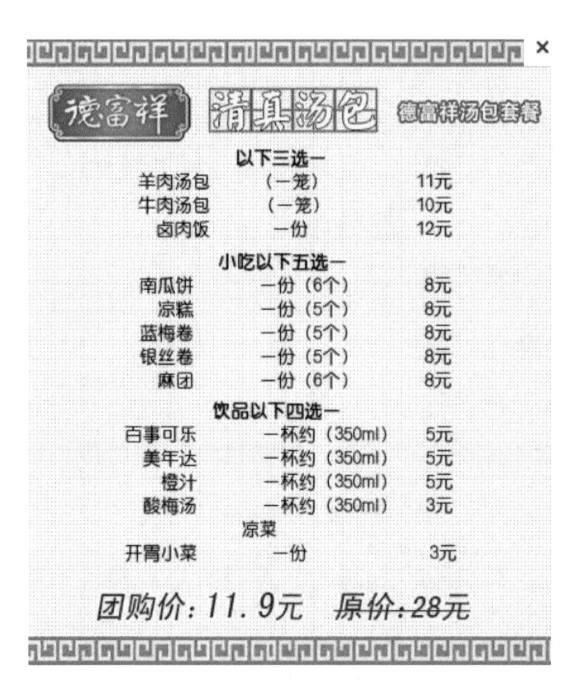

德富祥 清真汤包　德富祥汤包套餐

以下三选一

羊肉汤包	（一笼）	11元
牛肉汤包	（一笼）	10元
卤肉饭	一份	12元

小吃以下五选一

南瓜饼	一份（6个）	8元
凉糕	一份（5个）	8元
蓝梅卷	一份（5个）	8元
银丝卷	一份（5个）	8元
麻团	一份（6个）	8元

饮品以下四选一

百事可乐	一杯约（350ml）	5元
美年达	一杯约（350ml）	5元
橙汁	一杯约（350ml）	5元
酸梅汤	一杯约（350ml）	3元

凉菜

开胃小菜	一份	3元

团购价：11.9元　　原价：28元

Character Notes 汉字讲解

1. 火字旁

The 'fire radical' implies 'fire.' For example:

炒	chǎo	v	to stir-fry
爆	bào	v	to explode
炸	zhá	v	to deep-fry
烧	shāo	v	to burn
点	diǎn	v	to light up; to point; to order food
蒸	zhēng	v	to steam

2. 绞丝旁

The 'silk radical' implies 'fabric.' For example:

线	xiàn	n	thread
红	hóng	adj	red
绿	lǜ	adj	green

3. 示字旁

The 'show radical' originates from ancient workshipping or fortune-telling. For example:

福	fú	n	fortune
社	shè	n	organized body
礼	lǐ	n	ritue; manners

4. 饭字旁

The 'food radical' implies 'to eat' or 'food.' For example:

饭	fàn	n	food; meal
馆	guǎn	n	hall; restaurant
饮	yǐn	v	to drink

Grammar and Usage 语法讲解

1. The Chinese way of saying the day of the week is 星期 (xīngqī), 礼拜(lǐbài), or 周 plus a number except for 'Sunday.' Here are days of the week in Chinese:

星期一	礼拜一	周一	Monday
星期二	礼拜二	周二	Tuesday
星期三	礼拜三	周三	Wednesday
星期四	礼拜四	周四	Thursday
星期五	礼拜五	周五	Friday
星期六	礼拜六	周六	Saturday
星期天	礼拜日	周日	Sunday

2. 一边...一边... is placed before two verbs to indicate that two actions are taking place at the same time. For example:
   1) 她一边弹钢琴，一边唱歌。She is playing the piano and singing at the same time.
   2) 他们一边走，一边聊天。They are walking and chatting at the same time.
   3) 学生们一边学习，一边工作。Students study and work at the same time.

Cultural Information 文化常识

1. There exist eight famous regional cuisines 八大菜系 in China. They are Lu, Yue, Chuan, Xiang, Min, Nan, Su, and Wan. 鲁菜 (lǔcài), famous for its cabbage and long scallion, originates in Shandong Province. 粤菜 (yuècài), known for its seafood and freshness, originates from Guangdong Province. 川菜 (chuāncài) and 湘菜 (xiāngcài), famous for their hot and spicy foods, respectively came from Sichuan Province and Hunan Province. 闽菜(mǐncài), known for its thin slices, comes from Fujian Province. 南菜, (náncài), famous for its sweet and sour fish, originates in Zhejiang Province. 苏菜(sūcài), also known for its freshness, comes from Jiangsu Province. 徽菜 ((huī cài), famous for its colors, originates in Anhui Province.

2. 奶茶 'milk tea'
   Traditionally, Han Chinese drink their tea plain. However, under the influence of the British afternoon tea, tea served with milk and sugar became popular in Hong Kong. Later, in Taiwan, another kind of sweetened iced tea with milk was invented with black gummy balls made of tapioca added, giving rise to 'pearl milk tea'. This tea soon spread all over Asia and parts of America and Europe where Chinese populate. It is typically served cold in trended tea shops, not restaurants, as refreshments.

3. 早茶'morning tea,' also known as 'dim sum,' originated in Guangdong Province. Traditionally, Cantonese enjoy going to the tea house on weekends or holiday

mornings with their friends or families to sip tea and taste snacks as a pastime.
Morning tea features all kinds of tea as well as dozens if not hundreds of snacks.
The waiters and waitresses usually push around little carts full of various snacks for
customers to sample. As a custom, one should pour tea for other people on the table
before filling his/her own cup. To show gratitude, the one who receives the tea should
knock gently on the table with his/her index and middle knuckles while tea is served.
When Cantonese migrated to other parts of the world including North America, they
brought with them the custom of morning tea. Nowadays, morning tea can be found
in Chinatowns all over the country.

Pattern Drill 句型操练

Substitue the underlined parts in the following sentences with the expressions in the box.

1. 这就是我家开的中餐馆。

i. 我的父母亲
ii 你要的书
iii. 你点的菜

2. A: 您要喝什么茶？

   B: 我喜欢喝绿茶。

A. i.　喝什么　　B. i. 喝奶茶
ii.　吃什么　　ii. 水果
iii.　打什么球　iii. 打网球 (wǎngqiú, tennis)

3. 来两杯绿茶，一碟凤爪和一碟小菜。

i. 一杯咖啡　一份薯条(shǔtiáo, French fries)　一个汉堡包(hànbǎobāo, burger)
ii.　一杯红茶　一块蛋糕(dàngāo,cake)　　一碗面条(miàntiáo, noodle)
iii. 一盘炒粉　一盘炒饭　一碗汤(tāng, soup)

4. <u>这个清蒸龙利</u>真好吃。

> i. 块比萨饼 (bǐsàbǐng, pizza) 好吃
>
> ii. 盘炒粉　好吃
>
> iii. 碗皮蛋粥　好喝

5. 谢谢你请我<u>吃饭</u>。

> i. 看电影
>
> ii. 喝早茶
>
> iii. 去 KTV 唱歌

Pronunciation Drill 语音操练

Recite the classical poem 登鹳鹊楼 by 孟浩然 with the help of *pinyin*.

白日依山尽，	bái rì yī shān jìn
黄河入海流，	huáng hé rù hǎi liú
欲穷千里目，	yù qióng qiān lǐ mù，
更上一层楼。	gèng shàng yī céng lóu

Exercises 练习

1. Write the Chinese characters that correspond to the following words in *pinyin*.

1) shēngyì 3) xīnglóng 5) fúwùyuán 7) náshǒucài

2) xīngqītiān 4) hēchá 6) páiduì 8) pǐncháng

2. Match the words from the top line with words tha typically go with them on the bottom line.

生意　　　开　　　　有　　　五花　　　各式　　　品尝

餐馆　　　点心　　　兴隆　　　各样　　　八门　　　口福

3. Guess the meaning and sound of the following characters by breaking them down to their respective semantic and phonetic parts.

1）燃 = _____ + _____ sound: _____ meaning: _____

2）织 = _____ + _____ sound: _____ meaning: _____

3）祥 = _____ + _____ sound: _____ meaning: _____

4）馒 = _____ + _____ sound: _____ meaning: _____

4. Use the following characters to form two words and make a sentence for each of the words.

1) 菜　_____　_____

　　　　_____　_____

2) 客　_____　_____

　　　　_____　_____

3) 茶　_____　_____

　　　　_____　_____

4) 品　_____　_____

　　　　_____　_____

5. Fill in the blanks with the words given. You may use the same word more than once.

个　　　位　　　杯　　　碟　　　条　　　口

1) 我家有四_____人。

A: 请问，去中国城要过几_____街口？

B: 过三_____街就到了。

2) A: 请问，几_____？

B: 两_____。

3) 我要一_____奶茶，两_____小菜。

6. Translate the following sentences into Chinese.

1) Every weekend, I will go to Chinatown to have morning tea with my friends.
2) We are tasting morning tea and chatting at the same time.
3) There are all kinds of tea available at morning tea.
4) There is also a wide variety of snacks available.
5) My friends and I really have gourmet's luck.

7. Correct the mistakes in the following sentences.

1) 星期天所有的中餐馆都座满了人。
2) 大家一边喝茶和一边聊天。
3) 谢谢你请客我吃饭。
4) 下次你一定要来我家坐客。
5) 我的学校里没得喝茶。

8. Write a short paragraph (50-75 characters) about your favorite Chinese dish. Please specify its name, main ingredients, and steps in preparing the dish. Please explain why you like the dish.

9. Search online about dining etiquette in Chinese culture and be prepared to share your findings with the class.

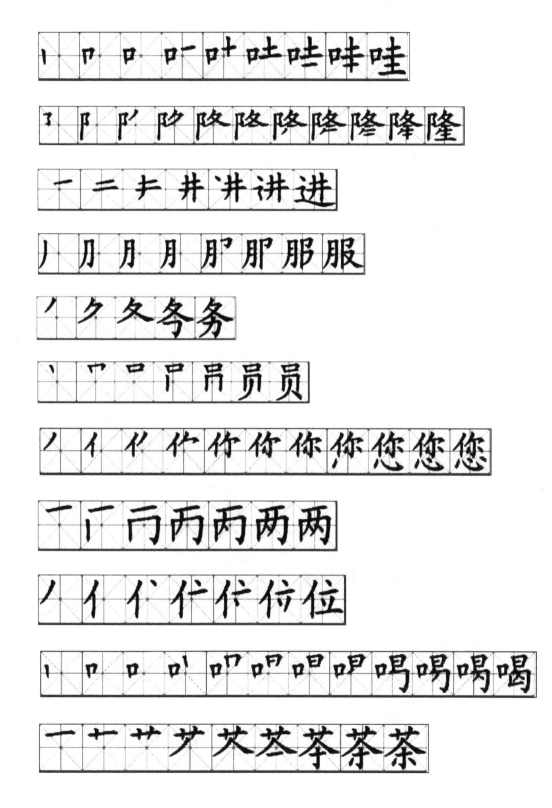

丨	口	口	叮	叶	吐	哇	哗	哇		
丨	阝	阝'	阵	陉	陉	隆	隆	隆	隆	隆
一	二	丰	井	讲	讲	进				
丿	几	月	月	肝	肝	那	服			
丿	夕	冬	条	务						
丶	吖	吖	吕	吊	员	员				
丿	亻	亻	乍	乍	你	你	你	您	您	您
一	厂	丙	丙	两	两	两				
丿	亻	亻	亻	仿	位	位				
丨	口	口	叮	咿	喝	喝	喝	喝	喝	喝
一	十	艹	艹	艾	苓	苶	茶	茶		

113

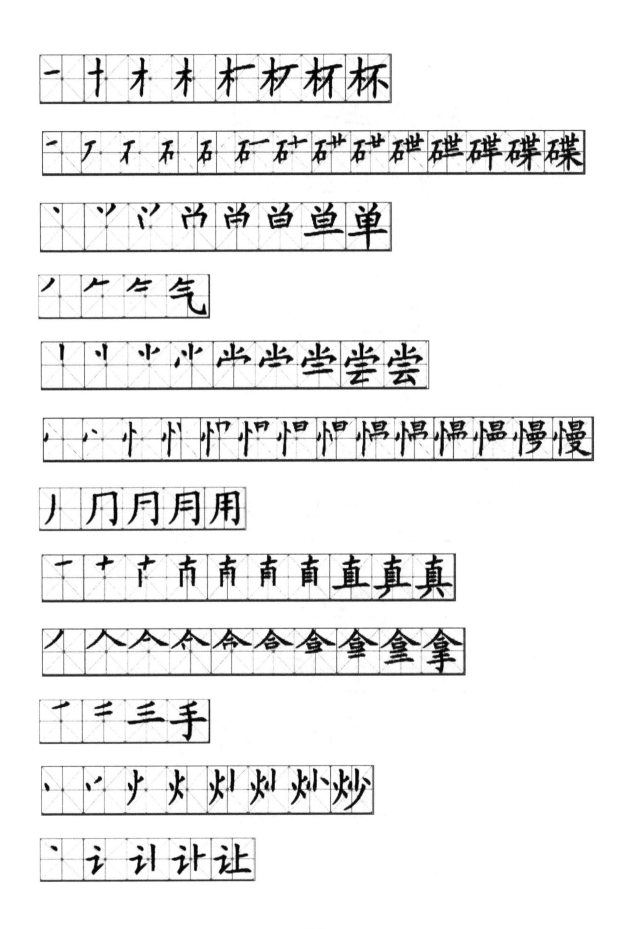

一 十 才 木 术 材 杯 杯

一 ア 石 石 石 石 矿 矿 砒 碟 碟 碟 碟

丶 丷 炒 兴 单 单 单

丿 仁 气 气

丨 丨 屮 屮 少 尚 堂 尝 尝

丶 丷 忄 忄 忙 忙 忙 慢 慢 慢 慢 慢

丿 门 月 月 用

一 十 古 古 南 南 南 直 真 真

丿 人 今 今 令 合 盒 盒 盒 拿

一 二 三 手

丶 丷 炒 火 灿 灿 炒 炒

丶 讠 计 计 让

114

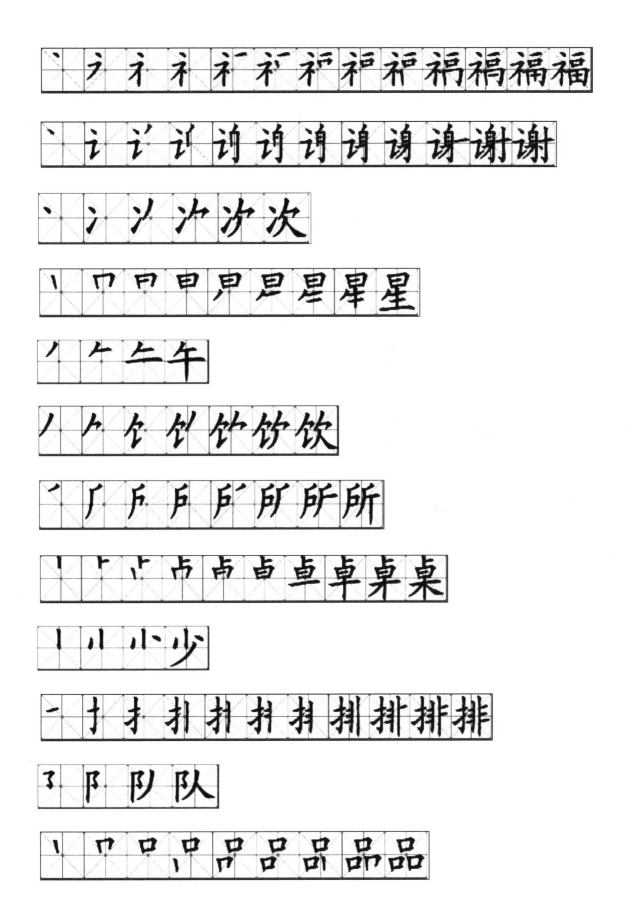

福　谢　次　星　午　饮　所　桌　少　排　队　品

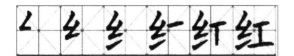

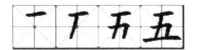

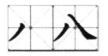

Lesson 8 第八课 Visiting a Friend's Family 在朋友家做客

Think and Share 想想说说

1. 去中国人家做客的时候，一般要带些什么礼物？When visiting a Chinese family, what kinds of presents do you usually bring?
2. 客人进主人家的时候要注意什么？What should the guest do when he/she enters the host's home?
3. 客人进屋以后，主人应该请客人做什么？After the guest enters the home, what should the host do?
4. 主人收到客人送的礼物，一般说什么客套话？When presented presents, what pleasantries does the host usually say?
5. 客人进了主人家，一般说什么客套话？When the guest enters the host's home, what pleasantries does the guest usually say?
6. 入座吃饭的时候，有没有什么讲究？What Chinese table manners should one observe?
7. 吃完饭以后，客人可不可以马上离开？When dinner is over, can the guest leave right away?
8. 客人离开的时候，主人应该做什么？When the guest is leaving, what should the host do?

Dialogue 对话

王丽莉：我家到了，请进。

陈凯文：伯父、伯母，您好！

王伯父：是凯文吧，快请进。

陈凯文：伯父、伯母，这是给您的一点小礼物。

王伯母：来了就好，怎么还带东西呢！

王丽莉：凯文，请坐吧。请喝茶。

陈凯文：谢谢。你们家真大、真漂亮呀。

王丽莉：哪里，只是两层楼而已。楼上是四个卧室和两个浴室，楼下是两个客厅、

　　　　一个厨房、和一个洗手间。

王伯父：凯文，来，尝尝伯母做的拿手菜。

陈凯文：哇，伯母的厨艺可真好。

王伯母：哪里，哪里，只是家常便饭而已。

王伯父：凯文，学校的饭菜你还吃得惯吗？

陈凯文：刚开始吃不惯，总是想家里的饭菜，不过现在习惯多了。

王丽莉：爸、妈，凯文还会自己做菜呢。

王伯母：是吗？那什么时候请凯文为我们做几道菜尝尝。

陈凯文：好呀，一言为定。

Answer Questions 回答问题

1. 陈凯文去谁家做客？Whose family did Kevin Chen visit?
2. 凯文进家以后，王丽莉请他做什么？After Kevin came in, what did Lily Wang offer him?
3. 王丽莉家有几间房？How many rooms are there in Lily Wang's home?
4. 陈凯文吃得惯还是吃不惯学校的饭菜？Is Kevin Chen used to school's food?

Vocabulary 生词

1.	伯父	bófù	n	uncle (father's older brother); friend's father
2.	伯母	bómǔ	n	aunt (wife of father's older brother); friend's Mother
3.	您	nín	pron	you (honorific; singular and plural)
4.	给	gěi	v	to give
5.	一点	yìdiǎn	adj	a little
6.	礼物	lǐwù	n	gift
7.	怎么	zěnme	adv	how; how come
8.	带	dài	v	to bring
9.	层	céng	m	story (of a building); layer
10.	而已	éryǐ	adv	that's all
11.	卧室	wòshì	n	bedroom
12.	浴室	yùshì	n	bathroom

13. 客厅	kètīng	n	living room
14. 厨房	chúfáng	n	kitchen
15. 洗手间	xíshǒujiān	n	restroom; powder room
16. 厨艺	chuyì	n	culinary art
17. 家常便饭	jiāchángbiànfàn	idiom	homely, simple meal; common occurence
18. 刚	gāng	adv	just about
19. 开始	kāishǐ	v	to begin
20. (习)惯	xíguàn	v/n	to get used to; habit
21. 现在	xiànzài	adv	now
22. 为	wèi	prep	for
23. 道	dào	n/m	course; (measure word for dish)

Short Reading 阅读短文

　　到中国人家做客，一般要准备一点小礼物，如水果、茶叶、或者地方特产等等。进门的时候，客人一定要脱鞋，换上主人给准备的拖鞋。中国人喜欢用茶点来招待客人，有时候也会留客人吃饭。吃饭的时候，要让长辈先入座、动筷，晚辈还应该给长辈夹菜，主人也会给客人夹菜，劝客人多吃一点。吃完饭以后，客人谢过主人，不要马上离开，应该帮着主人收拾碗筷，跟主人聊聊天才走。主人会送客人到门口，直到客人看不见了才关门。

Answer Questions 回答问题

1. 去中国人家做客，一般要带些什么小礼物？What small presents do Chinese people usually bring to visit someone?

2. 中国人一般用什么来招待客人？With what do Chinese people generally use to entertain their guest(s)?

3. 请客吃饭的时候，主人一般要为客人做什么？What do hosts usually do for their guests during dinner?

4. 吃完饭以后，客人一般要为主人做什么？After eating, what do guests usually offer to do for their hosts?

Vocabulary 生词

1.	准备	zhǔnbèi	v	to prepare
2.	如	rú	prep	such as; for example
3.	水果	shuǐguǒ	n	fruit
4.	茶叶	cháyè	n	dried tea leaves
5.	地方	dìfāng	adj/n	local; place
6.	特产	tèchǎn	n	special product
7.	客人	kèrén	n	guest
8.	脱鞋	tuōxié	v	take off shoes
9.	换上	huànshàng	v	to change into
10.	主人	zhǔrén	n	host
11.	拖鞋	tuōxié	n	slippers, sandals
12.	招待	zhāodài	v	to treat; to entertain
13.	留	liú	v	to stay behind; to keep (a guest)
14.	长辈	zhǎngbèi	n	older people; senior
15.	先	xiān	adv	first
16.	入座	rùzuò	v	take a seat
17.	动筷	dòngkuài	v	to start eating
18.	晚辈	wǎnbèi	n	younger people; junior
19.	应该	yīnggāi	aux	should
20.	夹菜	jiácài	v	to add food with chopsticks
21.	劝	quàn	v	to urge
22.	完	wán	v	to finish

23. 以后	yǐhòu	prep	after
24. 离开	líkāi	v	to leave
25. 马上	mǎshàng	adv	right away
26. 帮	bāng	v	to help
27. 收拾	shōushi	v	to clean up
28. 碗筷	wǎnkuài	n	bowls and chopsticks; empty dishes
29. 才	cái	adv	only then
30. 送	sòng	v	to send, to see someone off
31. 门口	ménkǒu	n	door
32. 直到	zhídào	conj	until
33. 看不见	kànbùjiàn	v	cannot be seen
34. 关	guān	v	to close

Task 1 Group /Class Activity 小组/全班活动

In a group of four, role-play the following situation: you are bringing your American boyfriend/girlfriend home to meet your Chinese parents for the first time and treat him/her to dinner. Create a conversation among the four characters to illustrate dos and don'ts of the Chinese custom related to visiting and dining. You may optionally present your skit to the whole class.

Task 2 Class Activity 全班活动

Watch segments of the movie <u>Joy Luck Club</u> as a class. Compare and contrast Chinese and American cultures in the area of hospitality. Feel free to cite examples from your own experience.

Character Notes 汉字讲解

1. 提手旁

The 'hand radical' implies 'hand.' For example:

换	huàn	v	to exchange

121

拖	tuō	v	to drag
拾	shī	v	to pick up
招	zhāo	v	to greet by hand
打	dǎ	v	to hit
排	pái	v	to line up

2. 竹字头

The 'bamboo radical' implies 'bamboo.' For example:

筷	kuài	n	chopstick
篮	lán	n	basket
等	děng	v	to wait

3. 石字旁

The 'stone radical' inplies 'stone.' For example:

碗	wǎn	n	bowl
碟	dié	n	plate

4. 力字旁

The 'power radical' implies 'strength' or 'power.' For example:

动	dòng	v	to move
劝	quàn	v	to advise
加	jiā	v	to add

Grammar and Usage 语法讲解

1. 只…而已 'only…that's all' is an expression used with a verb phrase at the end of a sentence to indicate whatever that is said in the sentence is insignificant. For example:
   1) 只是一点小礼物而已。(It) is only a small gift, that's all.
   2) 我只会说一点中文而已。I can only speak a little Chinese, that's all.
   3) 学校只有一个中国学生社团而已。There is only one Chinese student club, that's all.

2. 吃得惯 and 吃不惯 are potential verb constructions which mean respectively 'be able to' and 'not able to.' Structurally, they are composed of V+得+V or V+不+V. For example:
   1) 学校的饭你吃不吃得惯？Are you used to school's food or not?

122

2) 客人看不见了。The guests cannot be seen anymore.

3) 在中国城看得到中国电影。In Chinatown one can watch Chinese movies.

3. 过 is an experiential particle placed after a verb to indicate that the action has already happened or has been experienced before. For example:

1) 客人谢过主人，不要马上离开。After thanking the host, the guest should not leave right away.

2) 你去过中国吗？Have you ever been to China?

3) 我上过中文课。I have taken Chinese class before.

Cultural Information 文化常识

It is customary in Chinese culture to address elders such as your friends' grandparents or parents as if they were your own relatives to show respect. For instance, you will use the generic terms 爷爷奶奶 for seniors of your grandparents' age, 伯父伯母 for men and women about your parents' age but older than your parents, and 叔叔阿姨 for men and women about your parents' age but younger than your parents. If you are not sure of your friends' paretns age, it is generally advisable to call men 伯父 and women 阿姨.

Pattern Drill 句型练习

Substitute the underlined parts in the following sentences with phrases in the box.

1. A: 这是给您的一点小礼物。

   B：来了就好，怎么还带东西呢！

   B. i. 你真是太客气(kèqi, polite)了，谢谢

   ii. 让你破费(pòfèi, waste money)了，真不好意思 (bùhǎoyìsi, embarrassed)

   iii. 不用(yòng, need) 这么客气

2. A: 你们家真大、真漂亮呀。

   B：哪里，只是两层楼而已。

A. i. 你的日文说得真好。	B. i. 会说一点
ii. 谢谢你的礼物	ii. 一点小意思
iii. 你的厨艺可真好呀	iii. 家常便饭
iv. 你真的要我请你吃饭吗？	iv. 说说

3. 来，<u>尝尝伯母做的拿手菜</u>。

i. 看看我给你的礼物

ii. 聊聊你的大学生活

iii. 玩玩这个电子游戏

4. A: <u>学校的饭菜你吃得惯</u>吗？

   B: <u>刚开始吃不惯</u>。

A. i. 刚刚离开的客人	看得见	B. i. 看不见了
ii. 这么多的菜	吃得下	ii. 吃得下
iii. 走路去中国城	走得到	iii. 走不到
iv. 三杯奶茶	喝得了(liǎo)	iv. 喝得了

Pronunciation Drill 语音练习

Recite the following tongue twiser with the help of *pinyin*.

板凳宽，扁担长，	bǎn dèng kuān biǎn dan cháng
扁担绑在板凳上，	biǎn dan bǎng zài bǎn dèng shàng
板凳不让扁担绑在板凳上，	bǎn dèng bú ràng biǎn dan bǎng zài bǎn dèng shàng
扁担偏要绑在板凳上。	biǎn dan piān yào bǎng zài bǎn dèng shàng

Exercises 练习

1. Write the Chinese characters that correspond to the following words in *pinyin*.

    1) lǐwù   3) jiāchángbiànfàn   5) xíguàn   7) zhǔnbèi

    2) tèchǎn   4) zhāodài   6) wǎnbèi   8) shōushi

2. Match the words on the top line with their appropriate collocations on the bottom line.

    招待   收拾   入   动   送   夹

    碗筷   礼   菜   客人   座   筷

3. Guess the meaning and sound of the following characters by breaking them down to their respective semantic and phonetic parts.

    1) 把 = _____ + _____ sound: _____ meaning: _____

    2) 简 = _____ + _____ sound: _____ meaning: _____

    3) 砖 = _____ + _____ sound: _____ meaning: _____

    4) 功 = _____ + _____ sound: _____ meaning: _____

4. Use the following Chinese characters to form two compound words and make one sentence for each of the compound words.

    1) 礼   _____   _____

           _____   _____

    2) 菜   _____   _____

           _____   _____

125

3) 辈 _____ _____

_____ _____

4) 主 _____ _____

_____ _____

5. Fill in the blanks with the words given, using each word only once.

1) 着　　　　过

你有没有去_____中国城喝茶？

饮茶的时候，大家喝_____茶，吃_____点心。

2) 得　　　　不

A：从你家走_____到中国城吗？

B：我家离中国城太远，走路走_____到。

3) 拖鞋　　　　脱鞋

中国人进家要_____。

你有没有看见我的_____？

4) 要　　　　应该

去中国人家做客的时候，_____准备一点小礼物。

晚辈一定_____让长辈先入座、动筷。

6. Translate the following sentences into Chinese.

1) A: Please have a seat. Please have a cup of tea.
   B: Thank you. Your home is beautiful.
2) A: This is a little present for you.
   B: You shouldn't have.
3) A: Your cooking skill is great!
   B: Not at all. It's just some ordinary food, that's all.
4) A: Are you used to Chinese food?
   B: I wasn't used to at the beginning, but now I'm used to it.

7. Correct the mistakes in the following sentences.

    1) 谢谢你请我做客到你的家里。
    2) 吃饭的时候，主人要让客人先入坐。
    3) 中国人请客，主人总是劝客人吃多一点。
    4) 大家一边吃过东西，一边聊着天。
    5) 吃完饭以后，客人谢着主人才离开。

8. Write a short paragraph (50-75 characters) in which you describe your experience visting a friend's home.

9. Search online about Chinese etiquette vis-a-vis hospitality and be prepared to share your findings with the class.

Character Stroke Order 生字笔画

一 丁 丆 王 乒 臣 臤 卧

一 厂 厈 斤 斤 后 后 厔 厨 厨 厨

一 艹 艺

丨 冂 刀 冈 刚 刚

乀 女 女 妁 姇 始 始

丶 忄 忄 忄 怛 怛 惯 惯 惯 惯

丶 冫 冫 爿 爿 爿 爿 爿 准 准

丿 夂 夂 夂 各 各 备 备

乀 女 女 妁 如 如

亅 扌 水 水

丨 冂 曰 日 旦 早 果 果

丨 冂 口 叶 叶

丶 亠 产 产 立 产

丿 刀 月 月 月 朋 胪 胪 胪 脱

一 ナ 卄 卄 卄 芦 芇 苩 革 革 靳 靳 靳 靳 鞋

一 ナ 才 扌 扩 护 护 扬 换 换

一 ナ 才 扌 扩 拵 拖 拖

一 ナ 才 扌 扩 护 护 招 招

丿 夕 彳 彳 彳 彳 待 待 待

一 ｜ 匚 臼 臼 臼 留 留 留 留

丿 千 长 长

丿 ㇆ ㇆ ㅋ 非 非 非 非 韭 韭 韭

丿 亇 牛 先 先 先

丿 入

丿 丿 丿 丿 笁 笁 笁 笁 筲 筲 筲 筷 筷

丶 亠 广 广 庁 应 应

129

` 讠 讠 讠 讠 该 该 该

一 一 冖 亚 夹 夹

フ 又 刄 劝

丶 八 宀 宀 宀 完

一 二 三 丰 邦 邦 邦 帮 帮

丨 丩 丩 收 收 收

一 扌 扌 扑 扑 扒 拾 拾

一 丆 丆 石 石 矵 矿 矿 矿 碦 碗 碗

一 寸 才

丶 丷 丷 关 关 关 送 送

一 十 冇 市 市 直 直 直

丨 冂 贝 见

丶 丷 丷 兰 关 关

Unit Five 第五单元

My Hobbies 我的爱好

Lesson 9 第九课 Music 音乐

Think and Share 想想说说

1. 你喜不喜欢听音乐？Do you like to listen to music?
2. 你喜欢听什么音乐？What kind of music do you like to listen to?
3. 你最喜欢哪个音乐家？为什么？Who is your favorite musician? Why?

Dialogue 对话

陈凯文：哇，你的音乐 CD 可真多，可以开 CD 店了。

王丽莉：是呀，摇滚乐、爵士乐、节奏蓝调、乡村音乐、古典音乐，应有尽有。

陈凯文：你最喜欢什么音乐？

王丽莉：除了古典音乐以外，我最喜欢爵士乐。

陈凯文：你为什么喜欢古典音乐呢？

王丽莉：因为古典音乐是音乐之母，像莫扎特、贝多芬、肖邦，他们的音乐经久
    不衰。

陈凯文：那你为什么喜欢爵士乐呢？

王丽莉：我觉得爵士乐是美国的古典音乐，对后来的各种流行音乐有着重要的影
响。

陈凯文：你最喜欢哪首爵士乐？

王丽莉：我最喜欢 George Gershwin 的"夏日时光"，由 Ella Fitzgerald 和 Louis
    Armstrong 演唱，是爵士乐的经典作品。

陈凯文：除了美国的流行音乐以外，你听不听中国的流行音乐呢？

王丽莉：当然，只要是音乐我都喜欢。

陈凯文：那你最喜欢哪个中国流行音乐歌手呢？

王丽莉：应该是周杰伦吧。他的音乐结合了各种古典和现代流行音乐的长处，非常
    动听。

陈凯文：那下次周杰伦来美国开演唱会，我请你去听，好吗？

王丽莉：好呀，一言为定。

Answer Questions 回答问题

1. 王丽莉最喜欢什么音乐？为什么？What type of music does Lily Wang like the most? Why?
2. 除了古典音乐以外，王丽莉还喜欢什么音乐？为什么？Besides classical music, what other music does Lily Wang enjoy? Why?
3. 王丽莉最喜欢哪首歌？为什么？What's Lily Wang's favorite song? Why?
4. 王丽莉最喜欢哪个中国歌手？为什么？Which Chinese singer does Lily Wang like the most? Why?

Vocabulary 生词

1.	节奏	jiézòu	n	rhythm
2.	应有尽有	yīngyǒujìnyǒu	idiom	all encompassing
3.	古典	gǔdiǎn	a	classical
4.	之母	zhīmǔ	n	(arch.) mother of
5.	像	xiàng	prep	like; such as
6.	经久不衰	jīngjiǔbùshuāi	idiom	ever-lasting
7.	觉得	juéde	v	feel
8.	后来	hòulái	adv	later
9.	各种	gèzhǒng	a	all kinds of
10.	流行	liúxíng	a/v	popular; to be in vogue
11.	重要	zhòngyào	a	important
12.	影响	yǐngxiǎng	v/n	to influence; influence
13.	首	shǒu	m	(measure word for music)
14.	由	yóu	prep	by (somebody); from (some place or something)
15.	演唱	yǎnchàng	v	to sing; to perform

16.	经典	jīngdiǎn	a/n	classical; classics
17.	作品	zuòpǐn	n	composition
18.	歌手	gēshǒu	n	singer
19.	结合	jiéhé	v	to combine
20.	现代	xiàndài	a	modern; contemporary
21.	长处	chángchu	n	strength
22.	非常	fēicháng	adv	extremely
23.	听	tīng	v	to listen
24.	动听	dòngtīng	adj	melodious
25.	演唱会	yǎnchànghuì	n	concert

Proper Nouns 专有名词

1.	摇滚乐	yáogǔnyuè	Rock and Roll
2.	爵士乐	juéshìyuè	Jazz
3.	节奏蓝调	jiézòu lándiào	Rhythm and Blues
4.	乡村音乐	xiāngcūn yīnyuè	Country Music
5.	古典音乐	gǔdiǎn yīnyuè	Classical Music
6.	莫扎特	mòzhātè	Mozart
7.	贝多芬	bèiduōfēn	Bethoven
8.	肖邦	xiāobāng	Chopin
9.	夏日时光	xiàrìshíguāng	Summer Time
10.	流行音乐	liúxíng yīnyuè	Popular Music; Pop
11.	周杰伦	zhōujiélún	Jay Chou

Short Reading 阅读短文

流行音乐，又叫'通俗音乐，'最早来自于美国的爵士乐，后来又发展成蓝调、摇滚乐、乡村音乐、节奏蓝调、嘻哈、说唱等等。流行音乐的特点是通俗易懂、轻松活泼、容易被听众接受。通俗音乐不仅在美国流行，而且在全世界也非常流行。当今中国流行音乐歌手，像周杰伦、蔡依林、张惠妹等等，唱的都是通俗歌曲。

Answer Questions 回答问题

1. 流行音乐又叫什么音乐？What is 'pop music' also known as?
2. 流行音乐最早来自于什么音乐？Which music did popular music originate from?
3. 流行音乐有什么特点？What are the characteristics of popular music?
4. 当今流行的中国歌手唱的都是什么歌曲？What type of songs do today's Chinese popular singers sing?

Vocabulary 生词

1.	通俗	tōngsú	a	popular
2.	来自于	láizìyú	v	to come from
3.	发展	fāzhǎn	v/n	to develop; development
4.	成	chéng	v	to become
5.	特点	tèdiǎn	n	characteristics
6.	通俗易懂	tōngsúyìdǒng	a	easy to understand
7.	轻松活泼	qīngsōnghuópō	a	light and spirited
8.	容易	róngyì	a	easy
9.	被	bèi	co-v	by
10.	听众	tīngzhòng	n	audience
11.	接受	jiēshòu	v	to receiv; to accept
12.	不仅...而且...	bùjǐn...érqiě...	conj	not only...but also
13.	世界	shìjiè	n	world
14.	当今	dāngjīn	adv	at the present time; nowadays
15.	歌曲	gēqǔ	n	song

135

Proper Nouns 专有名词

1. 嘻哈   xīhā   Hip Hop

2. 说唱   shuōchàng   Rap

3. 蔡依林   cài yīlín   Jolin Cai

4. 张惠妹   zhāng huìmèi   Sherry Zhang

Task 1 Pair Activity 双人活动

Role-play the following situation. Your favorite singer is coming to town to give a concert. Invite and persuade your friend to go to see the concert with you.

Task 2 Class Activity 全班活动

Research and give a short talk about your favorite musician. Play an audio-visual clip of the musician's work in the background as part of your presentation. Optionally, you may sing a song in Mandarin Chinese on KTV.

Character Notes 汉字讲解

1 · 双人旁

The 'double person radical' implies 'walking slowly.' For example:

行	xíng	v	to walk
很	hěn	adv	very
街	jiē	n	street
得	dé	v	to obtain

2 · 尸字旁

The 'corpse radical' implies 'body.' For example:

展	hǎn	v	to extend
尽	jìn	adj	finished; exhausted
属	shǔ	v	to belong

3. 欠字旁

The 'lack radical' is found in a group of words whose common properties are unclear. For example:

歌	gē	n	song

欢	huān	adj	happy

4. 牛字旁

The 'ox radical' implies 'ox' or 'cow.' For example:

特	tè	adj	special
物	wù	n	object; animal

Grammar and Usage 语法讲解

1. 古典 and 经典 both mean 'classical' or 'classic' in English, but in Chinese, 古典 implies 'old' or 'ancient' whereas 经典 means 'the best of its kind.' For example:
古典音乐	Classical Music
古典文学	Classical Literature
经典作品	classic composition
经典著作	classic works

2. 流行 and 通俗 can be both translated into 'popular' in English, but 流行 means 'popular' in the sense of 'in vogue' whereas 通俗 means 'popular' in the sense of 'common.' In addition, 流行 can function as a verb whereas 通俗 can't. For example:
    1) 现在很流行 iphone. Iphone is very popular (in fasion) right now.
    2) 请你用通俗的语言来自我介绍一下。Please introduce yourself in everyday (common) language.

3. 来自(于) 'come from' is a formal way of saying '从…来.' For example:
    1) 我的父母来自中国广东。My parents come from Guangdong, China.
    2) 美国现代流行音乐来自于爵士乐。American modern popular music came from Jazz.
    3) 喝早茶的习惯来自(于)广东、香港。The custom of 'morning tea' came from Guangdong and Hong Kong.

4. 被 'by' is a co-verb found in the Chinese passive construction 被 +(N)+V, which means somebody or something is affected by the action of the verb. For example:
    1) 通俗音乐容易被听众接受。Pop music can be easily accepted by the audience.
    2) 不到月底，钱都被我花光了。Before the end of the month, all the money was spent by me.
    3) 客人会被主人留下来吃饭。The guest will be asked to stay for dinner by the host.

5. 由 is another co-verb used in the Chinese passive construction which means 'to be done by somebody' or ' to originate from.' Please be sure not to confuse it with 被. For example:

   1) 夏日时光是由 George Gershwin 作曲的。'Summer Time' is composed by George Gershwin.

      *夏日时光是被 George Gershwin 作曲的。

   2) 流行音乐是由爵士乐发展而来的。Popular music is evolved from Jazz.

6. 不仅…而且… 'not only…but also…' is a conjunction that is placed before two phrases of the same category to combine them into one sentence. It is often followed by 还 or 也 in the second clause. For example:

   1) 王丽莉不仅喜欢古典音乐，而且还喜欢现代流行音乐。Lily Wang not only enjoys classical music but also modern popular music.

   2) 我的社区不仅生活方便，而且邻居也很友好。In my neighborhood life is not only convenient, but my neighbors are also very friendly.

   3) 不仅中国人爱吃中餐，而且美国人也爱吃中餐。Not only do Chinese people love Chinese food, but American people also love Chinese cuisine.

Cultural Information 文化常识

中国流行音乐 'Chinese popular music'

Chinese popular music originated in Shanghai in the early 20th century under the influence of Western Jazz musicians like Buck Clayton. The leading figure of Chinese pop then was Lin Jinhui. During 1950s-70s, under the rule of the Chinese Communist Party, Chinese Pop disappeared from Mainland China for Hong Kong and Taiwan, where Cantonpop and Mandopop emerged subsequently. After China opened its door to the West in the 1980s, Chinese Pop returned to Mainland China along with the influence of pop artists from Hong Kong and Taiwan. Nowadays, Chinese Pop has branched into various genres such as Hip Hop, Rap, Rock, and Punk Rock, etc.

Pattern Drill 句型操练

Substitute the underlined parts in the following sentences with the expressions in the box.

1. A: 除了美国的流行音乐以外，你听不听中国的流行音乐呢？

   B：只要是音乐我都喜欢。

A. i. 台球	你还喜欢打什么球	B. i. 打球
ii. 中餐	你喜不喜欢吃西餐	ii. 吃饭
iii. 奶茶	你还喜欢喝什么茶	iii. 茶
iv. 中文课	你喜不喜欢英文课	iv. 语言(yǔyán, language)课

2. 流行音乐最早来自于美国的爵士乐。

i. 美式(měishì, American Style)中餐	广东菜
ii. 电子游戏	纸板(zhǐbǎn, board)游戏
iii. 美国的华人(huárén, Chinese)移民	广东台山

3. 流行音乐容易被听众接受。

i. 你点的菜都	我吃完了
ii. 爸妈给我的钱都	我花光了
iii. 停车场都	别人(biérén, others)停满了

4. "夏日时光"是由 Ella Fitzgerald 和 Louis Armstrong 演唱的。

i. 喝早茶的习惯		广东人带到美国来
ii. 我的社区		很多街区组成(zǔchéng, form)
iii. 中国城	主要	中国来的新移民组成

139

5. 通俗音乐不仅在美国流行，而且在全世界也非常流行。

i. 他的父母	有钱	人	很好
ii. 我的街区	很美	邻居	很友好
iii. 早茶的点心	品种很多	价钱(jiàqian, price)	很好

Exercises 练习

1. Write the Chinese characters that correspond to the words in *pinyin* below.

    1) liúxíng　　　3) jīngjiǔbùshuāi　　5) yīngyǒujìnyǒu　　7) yǎnchàng

    2) fāzhǎn　　　4) tōngsúyìdǒng　　6) qīngsōnghuópō　　8) jiēshòu

2. Match the words on the top line with the words that typically go with them on the bottom line.

    经典　　　经久　　　通俗　　　轻松　　　演唱　　　应有　　　来自　　　发展

    易懂　　　作品　　　歌曲　　　尽有　　　不衰　　　于　　　成　　　活泼

3. Guess the meaning and sound of the following characters by breaking them down to their respective semantic and phonetic parts.

    1) 径 = _____ + _____ sound: _____ meaning: _____

    2) 屎 = _____ + _____ sound: _____ meaning: _____

    3) 次 = _____ + _____ sound: _____ meaning: _____

    4) 牲 = _____ + _____ sound: _____ meaning: _____

4. Use the following characters to form two compound words and make a sentence with each of them.

1) 来 _____ _____

_____ _____

2) 典 _____ _____

_____ _____

3) 唱 _____ _____

_____ _____

4) 听 _____ _____

_____ _____

5. Fill in the blanks with the words given, using each one only once.

1) 由　　被

美式中餐是_____广东菜发展而来的。

美式中餐已经_____很多美国人接受了。

2) 通俗　流行

当今中国_____周杰伦的音乐。

周杰伦是中国的_____歌手。

3) 经典　古典

'夏日时光'是爵士乐的_____作品。

_____音乐是现代 (modern) 音乐之母。

4) 发展成　　来自于

流行音乐最早_____美国的爵士乐，后来_____当今的各种通俗音乐。

141

6. Translate the following sentences into Chinese.

   1) There are really a lot of books in the library, all encompassing.
   2) The classical compositions by Bethoven are ever-lasting.
   3) Confucius is not only influential in China, but also in the whole world (全世界).
   4) American-style Chinese food combines the characteristics of Chinese cuisine and American cuisine.

7. Correct mistakes in the following sentences.

   1) '夏日时光' 是被 George Gershwin 作曲的。
   2) 周杰伦是中国当今最通俗的歌手。
   3) 贝多芬是经典音乐家。
   4) 我喜欢不仅中国音乐，而且美国音乐。

8. Write a sentence by using each of the words given below.

   1) 经久不衰：_____

   2) 通俗易懂：_____

   3) 应有尽有：_____

   4) 轻松活泼：_____

   5) 不仅…而且…：_____

9. Write a short paragraph (about 50-75 characters) introducing your favorite musician(s). Please include his/her name, home country, type of music, its characteristics, representative works, and explain why you like him/her.

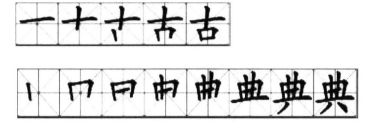

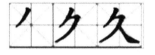

一 十 十 古 古

丨 冂 日 由 曲 曲 典 典

フ コ 尸 尺 尽 尽

丶 亠 之

丿 夕 久

丶 亠 广 市 庐 亩 亭 亵 衰

一 厂 厂 斤 后 后

丶 冫 氵 汁 沪 泸 泸 济 流

丿 彳 彳 行 行 行

一 二 千 市 市 盲 車 重 重

丨 冂 口 叮 听 哃 响 响

丶 丷 丷 光 光 芢 肖 首

143

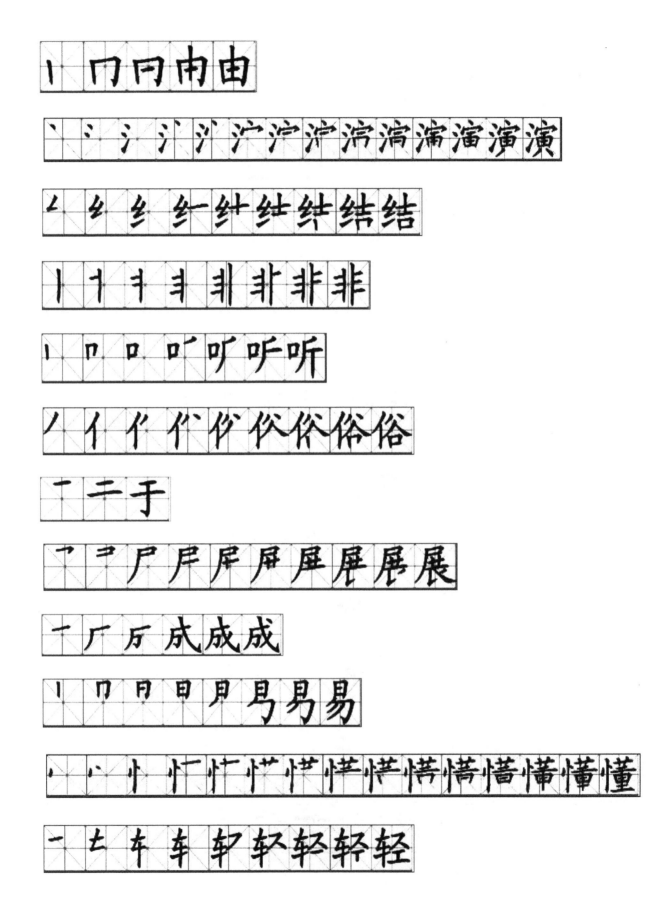

一 十 オ 木 朳 松 松 松

丶 冫 氵 汁 汫 泼 泼 泼

丶 宀 宀 宀 宀 突 突 容 容

丶 ァ ォ ネ 衤 衤 礻 衤 被 被

丿 个 个 众 夯 众

一 十 扌 扩 扩 扩 护 护 挐 接 接

丆 乀 乀 乊 灬 严 学 受

丿 亻 仅 仅

丨 刀 月 月 且

丨 冂 冃 両 曲 曲

Lesson 10 第十课 Shopping 购物

Think and Share 想想说说

1. 你喜欢逛商场吗？Do you like window shopping?
2. 你最喜欢逛哪一类的商店？Which kind of stores do you like to shop in most?
3. 你喜欢上网冲浪吗？为什么？Do you like to surf the internet? Why?
4. 上网冲浪有什么好处和坏处？What are the pros and cons of surfing the internet?

Dialogue 对话

王丽莉：凯文，怎么这么巧，在这里碰到你？你也喜欢逛商场吗？

陈凯文：我只是偶尔逛逛而已。你经常来逛街吗？

王丽莉：是的，我差不多每个星期天喝完早茶以后都会来逛逛。

陈凯文：你喜欢逛什么商店？

王丽莉：我喜欢逛时装店，看看有什么新款的时装，好像衣服、牛仔裤、裙子、鞋子、帽子、围巾、首饰等等。你呢？

陈凯文：我更喜欢逛电子城。看看有什么最新的电子产品，好像 ipad，ipodtouch，iphone 等等。

王丽莉：你最喜欢玩的是什么电子游戏？

陈凯文：不一定，什么游戏我都喜欢，特别是最新的游戏。

王丽莉：你这么喜欢玩电子游戏，会不会影响功课呀？

陈凯文：会的。我经常玩到夜里两、三点钟才睡觉，第二天上课直打瞌睡。

王丽莉：那你为什么还这么喜欢玩游戏？

陈凯文：因为玩游戏很放松，还可以锻炼大脑呢。电子城到了，你要不要跟我一起进去看看？

王丽莉：好呀，不过逛完电子城以后，你要陪我逛时装店，好吗？

陈凯文：没问题。

Answer Questions 回答问题

1. 王丽莉喜欢逛什么商店？What kind of stores does Lily Wang like to shop in?
2. 陈凯文喜欢逛什么商店？What kind of stores does Kevin Chen like to shop in?
3. 玩电子游戏有什么好处？What are some advantages of playing video games?
4. 玩电子游戏有什么坏处？What are some disadvantages of playing video games?

Vocabulary 生词

1.	巧	qiǎo	a	coincidental
2.	这里	zhèli	adv	here
3.	碰到	pèngdào	v	to run into
4.	逛	guàng	v	to stroll; to wander
5.	商场	shāngchǎng	n	mall; shopping center
6.	偶尔	ǒuěr	adv	occasionally
7.	差不多	chàbùduō	adv	almost
8.	时装	shízhuāng	n	fashionable clothing
9.	新款	xīnkuǎn	a	new-styled; fashionable
10.	衣服	yīfu	n	clothes; shirt or blouse
11.	牛仔裤	niúzǎikù	n	jeans
12.	裙子	qúnzi	n	skirt; dress
13.	帽子	màozǐ	n	hat
14.	围巾	wéijīn	n	scarf
15.	首饰	shǒushì	n	jewelry; accessory
16.	更	gèng	adv	even more
17.	电子	diànzǐ	a	electronic
18.	产品	chǎnpǐn	n	product

19. 好像	hǎoxiàng	prep	like; such as
20. 游戏	yóuxì	n	game
21. 功课	gōngkè	n	homework; schoolwork
22. 第	dì		(prefix for ordinal number)
23. 夜	yè	n	night; eve
24. 钟	zhōng	n	clock; o'clock
25. 睡觉	shuìjiào	v	to sleep
26. (一)直	(yì)zhí	adv	all the time
27. 打瞌睡	dǎkēshuì	v	to feel drowsy; to doze off
28. 放松	fàngsōng	v/a	to relax; relaxing; relaxed
29. 锻炼	duànliàn	v/n	to exercise; exercise
30. 大脑	dànǎo	n	brain
31. 陪	péi	v	to accompany; to keep someone's company

Short Reading 阅读短文

上网冲浪，又称"网上冲浪"，意思是在互联网上交流信息、获取服务、娱乐等等。随着高科技的发展，越来越多的人用电脑上网冲浪，在网上寻找信息、购物、听音乐、看电视、与朋友聊天等等，各种活动应有尽有、非常方便，是年轻人最时尚的娱乐方式。但是，网上冲浪也很浪费时间，而且不太安全，所以年轻人上网要适可而止，注意安全。

Answer Questions 回答问题

1. 什么是'上网冲浪'？What is 'surfing the internet'?
2. 人们在网上可以做些什么？What do people do on the internet?
3. 网上冲浪有什么好处？What are the advantages of surfing the internet?
4. 网上冲浪有什么坏处？What are the disadvantages of surfing the internet?

Vocabulary 生词

1.	上网	shàngwǎng	v	to go on the internet
2.	冲浪	chōnglàng	v	to surf
3.	称	chēng	v	to be known as
4.	网上	wǎngshang	a/adv	online; on the internet
5.	意思	yìsi	n	meaning
6.	互联网	hùliánwǎng	n	internet
7.	交流	jiāoliú	v	to exchange
8.	信息	xìnxī	n	information
9.	获取	huòqǔ	v	to obtain
10.	娱乐	yúlè	v/n	to entertain; entertainment
11.	随着	suízhe	prep	along with
12.	高	gāo	a	high; tall
13.	科技	kējì	n	science and technology
14.	越来越	yuèláiyuè	adv	more and more
15.	寻找	xúnzhǎo	v	to seek; to search
16.	电视	diànshì	n	television
17.	购物	gòuwù	n/v	to shop; shopping
18.	与	yǔ	prep	with; and
19.	年轻人	niánqīngrén	n	young people; youths
20.	时尚	shíshàng	n	fashion; fad
21.	方式	fāngshì	n	means; method
22.	浪费	làngfèi	v	to waste

23. 适可而止 shìkě'érzhǐ   idiom   to know when to stop

24. 注意   zhùyì   v   to pay attention

Task 1 Pair Activity 双人活动

Pair up with a partner and role-play bargaining. One person pretends to be the shopper and the other the seller.

Task 2: Group Activity 小组活动

Form two teams in a group and debate about the pros and cons of surfing the internet.

Character Notes 汉字讲解

1) 光字头

The "light radical' is found in a group of characters that sound like 光 'light.'
For example:

尝	cháng	v	to taste
常	cháng	adv	often
堂	táng	n	large room
尚	shàng	v	to value

2) 目字旁

The 'eye radical' implies 'eye.' For example:

看	kàn	v	to look
瞌睡	kēshuì	v	to take a nap; to feel drowsy
眼睛	yǎnjing	n	eye

3) 衣字旁

The 'clothing radical' implies 'clothing.' For example:

裙	qún	n	skirt; dress
被	bèi	n/co-v	quilt; by

4) 反文旁

The 'reverse language radical' implies 'language.' For example;

教	jiāo	v	to teach

150

放	fàng	v	to release
数	shǔ/shù	v/n	to count; number

Grammar and Usage 语法讲解

1. 差不多 'almost' is often used in comparison indicating that there is little difference. For example:

   1) 我跟你差不多，喜欢逛商场、购物。Like you, I enjoy shopping at the mall.
   2) 我家差不多每个周末都去中国城喝茶。My family goes to Chinatown for morning tea almost every weekend.

2. 才 'only then' is an adverb that is placed before a verb to indicate lateness or delay of the action. For example:
   1) 我玩到夜里一、两点钟才睡觉。I play until one or two o'clock at night before going to bed.
   2) 你怎么现在才起床？Why did you wake up just now?
   3) 你得做完功课才可以玩电子游戏。You must finish doing your homework before playing video games.

   就 'then', in contrast with 才, indicates the earliness or immediacy of an action. For example:

   1) 我每天晚上十点钟就睡觉了。I go to bed as early as 10 o'clock every night.
   2) 你怎么这么早就起床了？Why did you wake up so early?
   3) 我一做完功课就可以玩电子游戏了。As soon as I finish doing my homework, I can play video games.

3. 越来越 'more and more' is placed before a phrase to indicate a gradual change. For example:
   1) 现在越来越多人上网购物了。Now more and more people shop online.
   2) 物价越来越贵了。Prices are going up.
   3) 我越来越不喜欢逛街了。I dislike window shopping more and more.

Pattern Drill 句型操练

Substitute the underlined parts in the following sentences with the expressions in the box.

1. A: 你经常来逛街吗？

   B: 是的，我差不多每个星期天喝完早茶以后都会来逛逛。

A. i. 喝早茶	B. i. 每个周末	去中国城喝早茶
ii. 上网冲浪	ii. 每天	上网冲浪
iii. 听音乐会	iii. 每个月(yuè, month)	听音乐会
iv. 去别人家做客	iv. 每个星期	去别人家做客

2. <u>我经常玩到夜里两、三点钟才睡觉</u>。

i. 每天上课前 (qián, before)	做功课
ii. 直到现在 (xiànzài, now)	知道(zhīdào, know) 你叫什么名字
iii. 上大二后 (hòu, after)	知道自己要念什么专业
iv. 开车开了两个小时	到中国城

3. 越来越多的<u>人用电脑上网冲浪</u>。

i. 美国人开始学中文了
ii. 年轻人迷 (mí, addicted) 上了电子游戏
iii. 人在网上寻找自己想要的信息
iv. 大学生在网上上课

Exercises 练习

1. Write the Chinese characters that correspond to the words in pinyin below.

1) yóuxìjī   3) shuì jiào   5) guàng   7) duànliàn   9) wèntí ⊠

2）yì sī   4）yúlè   6）suízhe   8）kējì   10）làng fèi

2. Match the words on the top line with words that typically go with them on
    the bottom line.

锻炼   打   获取   随着   影响   交流

服务   功课   瞌睡   大脑   信息   发展

3. Guess the meaning and sound of the following characters by breaking them down to
    their respective semantic and phonetic parts.

    1) 党 = _____ + _____ sound: _____ meaning: _____

    2) 盲 = _____ + _____ sound: _____ meaning: _____

    3) 裤 = _____ + _____ sound: _____ meaning: _____

    4) 功 = _____ + _____ sound: _____ meaning: _____

4. Form two words with the characters given and then make one sentence by using one
    of each words.

    1) 商   _____   _____

            _____   _____

    2) 网   _____   _____

            _____   _____

    3) 电   _____   _____

            _____   _____

4) 睡　_____　_____

　　　　_____　_____

5. Fill in the blanks with words given, using each word only once.

1) 才　　就

陈凯文一有时间_____玩电子游戏。

他有时候一直玩到夜里一、两点钟_____睡觉。

2) 流行　时尚

当今世上 (in the world) 最_____iphone。

年轻人比较喜欢追求 (pursue) _____。

3) 网上　上网

做功课的时候，我喜欢_____寻找信息。

在_____可以做各种各样的活动，如购物、聊天、听音乐、看电视等等。

6. Write sentences by using the words given, one word for each sentence.

差不多：_____

随着：_____

越来越：_____

适可而止：_____

7. Translate the following sentences into Chinese.

1) Although online shopping is convenient, (but) one must pay attention to safety.
2) With the advance of high technology, more and more people go online to surf the internet.
3) Surfing the internet is the most popular means of entertainment among young people nowadays.
4) Not only can video games exercise the brain, but they can also affect school work.

8. Write a paragraph (50-75 characters) about your favorite pastime. Explain what it is, how you pursue it, and why you like it. You may be asked to share this in class.

Character Stroke Order 生字笔画

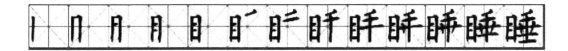

丨 丨 丬 丬 屵 尚 尚 尚

乚 女 女 奵 妒 妒 妒 娯 娛 娱

一 丁 工 功 功

一 十 士 吉 吉 寺 寿 素 素 款 款 款

1	2	3	4	5	6	7	8	9	10	11	12	13
一	丆	丆	石	石	石	矿	砬	砬	砬	砬	碰	碰

1	2	3	4	5
一	丁	工	工	巧

1	2	3	4	5	6	7	8	9	10
丿	犭	犭	犭	狂	狂	狂	狂	逛	逛

1	2	3	4	5	6	7	8	9	10	11
丿	亻	亻	们	但	但	偊	偶	偶	偶	

1	2	3	4	5
丿	仁	尔	尔	尔

1	2	3	4	5	6	7	8	9	10	11	12
丶	丬	壮	壮	壮	壮	壮	装	装	装	装	装

1	2	3	4
丿	丄	牛	牛

1	2	3	4	5
丿	亻	仔	仔	仔

丶	礻	礻	礻	礻	衤	衤	袢	裤	裤	裤	裤

丶	礻	礻	礻	礻	礻	衤	衤	袢	裙	裙	裙

丨	冂	巾	巾	帆	帆	帽	帽	帽	帽	帽	帽

丨	冂	冃	同	同	韦	围

丨	冂	巾

丿	夂	𥫗	𥫗	竹	竹	饰	饰

一	厂	冋	冋	冋	更	更

一	丁	工	功	功

丶	亠	广	疒	疒	夜	夜	夜

丶	亠	宁	方	方	放	放	放

阝	阝	阝	阼	阼	陪	陪	陪	陪	陪

丨	冂	冈	冈	网

Unit Six 第六单元

Chinese Traditional Holidays 中国传统节日

Lesson 11 第十一课 Lunar New Year 农历新年

Think and Share 想想说说

1. 中国有哪些传统节日？What are some traditional Chinese holidays?
2. 农历新年一般在一年的什么时候？When does the lunar new year generally fall on in a year?
3. 你喜不喜欢过农历新年？为什么？Do you like to observe Lunar New Year?
4. 你家是怎样过农历新年的？How does your family celebrate Lunar New Year?
5. 华人社区一般是怎样庆祝农历新年的？How do Chinese communities generally celebrate Lunar New Year?

Dialogue 对话

陈凯文：新年好！

王丽莉：恭喜发财！

陈凯文：丽莉，你的农历新年过得好吗？

王丽莉：很好。除夕夜里，我的哥哥姐姐都回家了，大家一边包饺子，一边聊天，
　　　　可开心了。你的春节过得好吗？

陈凯文：也很好。大年初一，我们全家人一起去中国城吃了一顿团圆饭，
　　　　还看了舞狮和放鞭炮，热闹极了。

王丽莉：你有没有收到红包？

陈凯文：当然有。我收到了十几个红包，有爷爷奶奶、爸爸妈妈给的，还有其他亲
　　　　戚给的，一共有两百五十块钱呢。你收到了几个红包？

王丽莉：我只收到了四个红包，是爸爸妈妈、哥哥姐姐给的，一共一百块钱。够我
　　　　买一套新衣服了。你打算怎么花你的压岁钱呢？

陈凯文：我打算花五十块钱来买一个新的电子游戏，剩下的两百块钱存进银行里。

王丽莉：你倒是蛮会省钱的。

陈凯文：是呀，我打算用自己存下来的钱做头款，开一家公司。

王丽莉：那我祝你新年快乐、心想事成！

陈凯文：谢谢，也祝你新年快乐、万事如意！

Answer Questions 回答问题

1. 王丽莉家是怎样过农历新年的？How does Lily Wang's family celebrate Lunar New Year?
2. 陈凯文家是怎样过农历新年的？How does Kevin Chen's family celebrate Lunar New Year?
3. 王丽莉收到了多少压岁钱？她打算怎样花她的压岁钱？How much lucky money does Lily Wang receive? How does she plan to spend her lucky money?
4. 陈凯文收到了多少压岁钱？他打算怎样花他的压岁钱？How much lucky money does Kevin Chen receive? How does he plan to spend his lucky money?

Vocabulary 生词

1.	传统	chuántǒng	a/n	traditional; tradition
2.	节日	jiérì	n	holiday; festival
3.	农历	nónglì	n	lunar calendar
4.	新年	xīnnián	n	new year
5.	恭喜发财	gōngxǐfācái	idiom	wishing you a prosperous new year
6.	除夕	chúxī	n	eve
7.	回家	huíjiā	v	to go home
8.	包	bāo	v	to wrap
9.	饺子	jiǎozi	n	Chinese dumpling
10.	可	kě	adv	quite; very
11.	春节	chūnjié	n	Spring festival; Chinese Lunar New Year
12.	大年	dànián	n	New Year
13.	初一	chūyī	n	first day of the month/year
14.	顿	dùn	m	(measure for meals)

15. 团圆饭	tuányuánfàn	n		family reunion dinner
16. 舞狮	wǔshī	n		lion dance
17. 放	fàng	v		to set off; to place
18. 鞭炮	biānpào	n		firecrackers
19. 极	jí	adv		extremely
20. 收到	shōudào	v		to receive
21. 红包	hóngbāo	n		red envelope
22. 亲戚	qīnqi	n		relative
23. 一共	yīgòng	adv		altogether
24. 块	kuài	n		measure word for 'dollar'
25. 够	gòu	adv		enough
26. 套	tào	m		(measure word for 'clothes', 'apartment', and things that uaually come in a set)
27. 打算	dǎsuàn	v		to plan
28. 压岁钱	yāsuìqián	n		lucky money
29. 剩下	shèngxià	v		leftover
30. 存	cún	v		to deposit
31. 银行	yínháng	n		bank
32. 倒是	dàoshì	adv		(colloq) ironically; unexpectedly
33. 省钱	shěngqián	v		to save money
34. 头款	tóukuǎn	n		front money
35. 公司	gōngsī	n		company
36. 存下来	cúnxiàlái	v		to save up
37. 祝	zhù	v		to wish
38. 快乐	kuàilè	a		happy
39. 心想事成	xīnxiǎngshìchéng		idiom	all your wishes come true

40. 万事如意　　　　　wànshìrúyì　　　　　idiom　everything goes your way

Short Reading 阅读短文

　　农历新年是农历的大年初一，也叫春节，是中国最重要的传统节日。新年的前一个星期，人们就开始打扫房间，张灯结彩，购买年货，准备过年。除夕夜里，外出的家人都要赶回家来吃团圆饭，一起守夜。大年初一，晚辈要给长辈拜年，长辈会给晚辈分红包。新年那天，中国城里还会放鞭炮、舞狮，十分热闹。我最喜欢过农历新年。

Answer Questions 回答问题

1. 农历新年又叫什么？What is Lunar New Year also known as?
2. 过新年人们都要做些什么准备？What preparations do people do for the Lunar New Year?
3. 除夕夜里人们一般做些什么？What do people usually do on Lunar New Year's Eve?
4. 大年初一人们一般都做些什么？What do people usually do on Lunar New Year's Day?

Vocabulary 生词

1.	前	qián	a	former; prior
2.	人们	rénmen	n	people
3.	打扫	dǎsǎo	v	to sweep and dust
4.	房间	fángjiān	n	room
5.	张灯结彩	zhāngdēngjiécǎi	idiom	to decorate with lanterns and paper cuts
6.	购买	gòumǎi	v	to purchase
7.	年货	niánhuò	n	goods for new year
8.	过年	guònián	v	to celebrate new year
9.	外出	wàichū	v	to travel outside
10.	家人	jiārén	n	family member

164

11. 赶	gǎn	v	to rush
12. 守夜	shǒuyè	v	to stay up all night
13. 拜年	bàinián	v	to wish happy new year
14. 分	fēn	v	to distribute
15. 十分	shífēn	adv	rather; quite

Task 1 Pair Activity 双人活动

Discuss with your partner how your family celebrates Chinese Lunar New Year. Compare and contrast the ways your families celebrate Chinese Lunar New Year.

Task 2 Group/Class Activity 小组/全班活动

Role-play the following scenes in groups of four. You may present your skit to the whole class.

Scene 1: You are preparing for Lunar New Year celebration a week before the holiday.
Scene 2: You are enjoying your family reunion dinner on Lunar New Year's Eve.
Scene 3: You greet each other on Lunar New Year's Day.

Character Notes 汉字讲解

1. 贝字旁

   The 'shell radical' implies 'money.' For example:

财	cái	n	wealth
购	gòu	v	to purchase
货	huò	n	merchandise
贵	guì	adj	expensive
费	fèi	n	fee

2. 立刀旁

   The 'standing knigh radical' implies 'cut.' For example:

剩	shèng	n	leftover; surplus
前	qián	a	former; prior
到	dào	v	to arrive
倒	dào	v	to reverse

3. 三撇旁

The 'three slant radical' classifies a group of words whose shared properties are unclear now. For example:

| 彩 | cǎi | n | color |
| 参 | cān | v | to partake |

4. 犬字旁

The 'dog radical' implies 'animal.' For example:

| 狮 | shī | n | lion |
| 猴 | hóu | n | monkey |

Grammar and Usage 语法讲解

1. 十几个 means 'over ten'. In Chinese, 几 means 'how many' in interrogative sentences or 'several' in affirmative sentences. A number + 几 means a few more than the number. 几+ a number means a few times of the number. For example:
   1) 你收到了几个红包？How many "red envelops" did you receive?
   2) 你们几个到这边来。You guys come over to this side.
   3) 我们中文班有二十几个学生。Our Chinese class has over twenty students.
   4) 我们学校有几百个中国学生。Our school has a few hundred Chinese students.

2. 倒是 is a colloquial expression placed before predicates indicating that whatever stated is rather unexpected. For example:
   1) 没想到你父母倒是蛮喜欢通俗音乐的。It's rather unexpected that your parents like popular music quite a lot.
   2) 我弟弟的中文倒是比我好。My little brother's Chinese is ironically better than mine.

Cultural Information 文化常识

农历新年 'Lunar New Year'

Lunar New Year, also known as 'Spring Festival', is one of the four most important traditional Chinese holidays. The holiday begins on the eve of New Year's Day on Chinese lunar calendar and ends with Lantern Festival 14 days later. As its name suggests, this holiday celebrates the beginning of spring and a new year . There are many lengends and festivities that go with this holiday. This holiday is widely celebrated not

166

only in China but also in other Asian countries like Korea, Vietnam, Singapore and Malaysia.

Pattern Drill 句型操练

Substitute the underlined parts in the following sentences with the expressions in the box.

1. <u>大家</u>一边<u>包饺子</u>, 一边<u>聊天</u>。

i. 我们	唱歌	跳舞 (tiàowǔ, dance)
ii. 客人们	喝茶	聊天
iii. 朋友们	说	笑 (xiào, laugh)
iv. 她	开车	听音乐

2. A: <u>你</u>有没有<u>收到红包</u>？

   B：当然有，<u>我收到了十几个红包</u>。

A.			B.	
i. 你们	看过中国电影		i. 我们看过很多中国电影	
ii. 你	听说过周杰伦		ii. 我还去听过他的演唱会呢	
iii. 你家	去过中国旅游 (lǚyóu, travel)		iii. 我家每年都去中国旅游	
iv. 他们	想过毕业后做什么		iv. 他们打算毕业后找工作	

3. A: 我打算<u>花五十块钱来买一个新的电子游戏，剩下的两百块钱存进银行里</u>。

   B：你倒是蛮<u>会省钱</u>的。

A.		B.	
i. 用自己存下来的钱做头款，开一家公司		i. 会打算	
ii. 花一百块钱，买套最新款的时装		ii. 会花钱	
iii. 送你一个生日礼物		iii. 有心	
iv. 打算每天让妈妈给我送饭来吃		iv. 有口福	

Exercises 练习

1. Write the Chinese characters that correspond to the following words in pinyin.

   1) gōngxǐfācái   3) xīnnián kuàilè   5) bàinián   7) chuántǒng

   2) xīnxiǎngshìchéng   4) wànshìrúyì   6) zhǔnbèi   8) zhòngyào

2. Match the words on the top line with words that typically go with them on the bottom line.

   舞   放   省   打扫   张灯   购买

   钱   房间   鞭炮   结彩   年货   狮

3. Guess the meaning and sound of the following characters by breaking them down to their respective semantic and phonetic parts.

   1) 账 = _____ + _____ sound: _____ meaning: _____

   2) 副 = _____ + _____ sound: _____ meaning: _____

   3) 衫 = _____ + _____ sound: _____ meaning: _____

   4) 猩 = _____ + _____ sound: _____ meaning: _____

4 · Make two compound words by using each of the following Chinese characters and then form a sentence by using each of the compound words.

   1）外 _____   _____

      _____   _____

   2）钱 _____   _____

      _____   _____

168

3) 包 _____ _____

_____ _____

4) 买 _____ _____

_____ _____

5. Fill in the blanks with the words given, one word for each blank.

一边，一边，倒是，十分，最，极，虽然，张灯结彩

_____ 我是在美国出生、美国长大的中国人，我_____非常

喜欢过农历新年。新年那天，中国城里到处_____，有人_____

舞狮_____放鞭炮，热闹_____了。我_____喜欢看花

(parade)，有各种各样的图案(design)，_____好看。

6. Translate the following sentences into Chinese.

1) Lunar New Year is the most important traditional holiday in China.
2) People begin to prepare for Lunar New Year a week before.
3) Family members who travel outside will return home for a family reunion dinner.
4) On New Year's Day, the younger generation will wish "Happy New Year" to the older generation.
5) The older generation will give "red envelops" to the younger generation.
6) I enjoy Lunar New Year the most.

7. Write a paragraph (75 -100 characters) about how your family celebrates Lunar New Year.

8. Go on the internet and search for legends and stories related to Chinese Lunar New Year. Please be prepared to share your finds with your classmates.

Character Stroke Order 生字笔画

ノ 亻 亻 仨 传 传

乙 纟 纟 纟 纣 纮 纮 统 统

丨 门 月 日

丶 亠 ⺈ 欢 农 农

一 十 卄 丗 井 共 丼 恭 恭 恭

丨 冂 贝 贝 贝 财 财

丨 冂 冂 冋 回 回

ノ 夕 夕

ノ 勹 勺 匀 包

ノ 𠆢 𠆢 𠆢 饣 饣 饣 饺 饺

一 二 三 夫 夫 表 春 春 春

丶 亠 礻 礻 礻 初 初

170

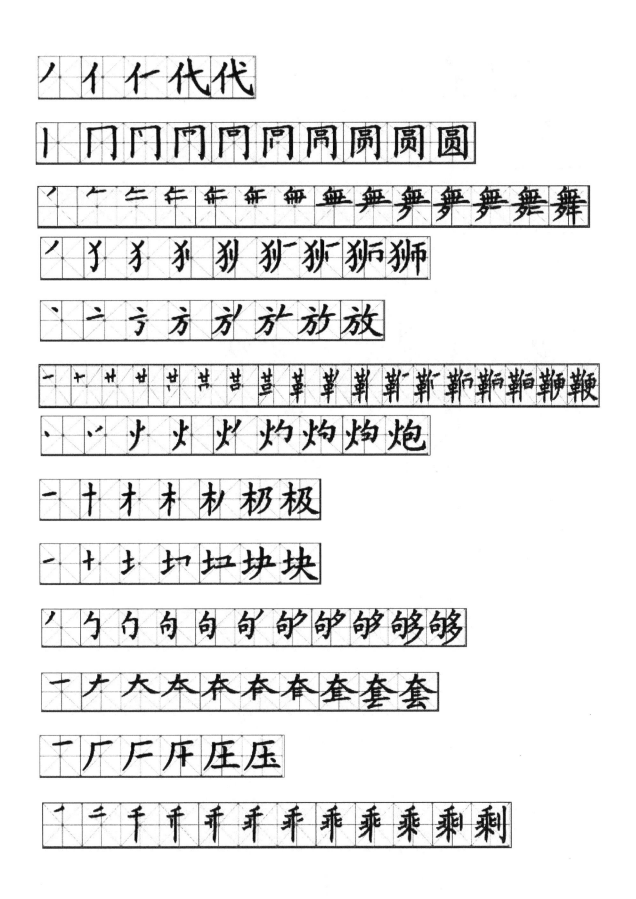

ノ イ 亻 代 代

丨 冂 冂 冂 冂 冋 囩 圆 圆 圆

ノ 广 仁 仁 牛 無 無 無 舞 舞 舞 舞 舞

ノ 犭 犭 犭 狉 狉 狮 狮 狮

丶 亠 亠 方 方 放 放 放

一 十 卄 卅 廿 苎 苫 苩 革 革 革 靬 靳 靮 靮 靮 鞭

丶 ソ 少 火 灯 灼 炮 炮 炮

一 十 才 木 朳 极 极

一 十 土 圹 圻 块 块

ノ 勹 勹 句 句 句 够 够 够 够

一 大 大 本 本 本 套 套 套 套

丆 厂 厂 厈 庄 压

丿 二 千 千 乒 乒 乒 乖 乖 乘 乘 剩 剩

171

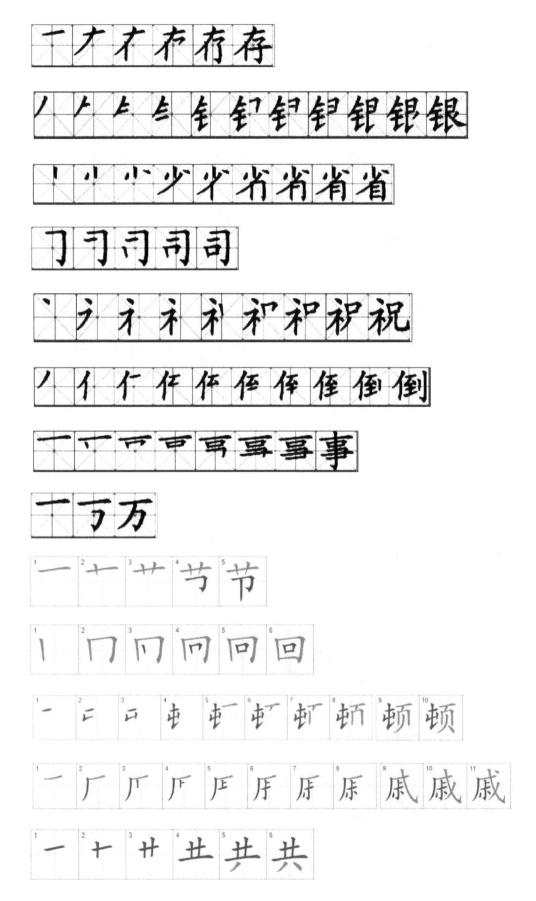

一 ナ オ 存 存 存

丿 ﹁ ﹂ 钅 钅 钅 钅 钅 银 银 银

⎸ ⎹ 小 少 少 半 省 省 省

⎾ ⎥ 司 司 司

丶 ｚ 礻 礻 礻 礻 礻 祝

丿 亻 亻 作 作 作 作 倒 倒 倒

一 丁 戸 申 写 写 事 事

一 丅 万

```
1       2       3       4       5
一      十      艹      节      节
```

```
1   2   3   4   5   6
⎸   冂   冋   同   回   回
```

```
1   2   3   4   5       6    7    8    9    10
一   ㄈ   ロ   申   虰   虰   虰   顿   顿   顿
```

```
1   2   3   4   5   6   7   8   9    10   11
一   厂   厂   厂   斤   斤   斥   咸   戚   戚
```

```
1   2   3   4    5   6
一   十   卄   共   共   共
```

172

⟍	⟍⟍	⺮	⺮	⺮	竹	笁	笴	筲	筲	筲	算	算	算

丿	八	公	公

丶	丷	丷	亠	亣	刖	刖	前	前

乛	弓	弓	弖	弚	张	张

丶	丷	少	火	灯

丿	勹	爫	爫	乯	平	采	采	彩	彩	彩

乛	乛	乛	丰	买	买

丿	亻	化	化	化	货	货	货

凵	凵	屮	出	出

一	十	土	丰	丰	走	走	走	走	赶

丶	宀	宀	宀	守	守

丿	二	三	手	手	手	拜	拜	拜

Lesson 12 第十二课 Mid-Autumn Festival 中秋节

Think and Share 想想说说

1. 中秋节一般在每年的什么时候？When does the Mid-Autumn Festival fall on in a year?
2. 你听说过什么有关中秋节的传说吗？Do you know of any legendary tales that go with the Mid-Autumn Festival?
3. 中秋节为什么要吃月饼？Why do Chinese people eat moon cakes for the Mid-Autumn Festival?
4. 你喜不喜欢吃月饼？为什么？How do you like the moon cake? Why?

Dialogue 对话

王丽莉：凯文，中秋节就要到了，你打算怎么过呀？

陈凯文：我的功课很忙，可能不回家了，就在学校过。你呢？

王丽莉：今年是我第一年离开家上大学，我还是想回家过中秋。

陈凯文：你家是怎样过中秋的？

王丽莉：我家一般会在中秋夜吃顿团圆饭，然后到院子里赏月，吃月饼。你呢？

陈凯文：我家也差不多，跟亲戚一起到中餐馆去吃顿团圆饭，当然也少不了吃月饼。

王丽莉：你喜欢吃月饼吗？

陈凯文：还好，就是太甜了。你呢？

王丽莉：我不太喜欢吃月饼，还是蛋糕比较好吃。你不回家过中秋，多没意思呀。

陈凯文：不会呀，中国学生会每年都会举办中秋晚会，有唱歌跳舞，还有东西吃，蛮热闹的。

王丽莉：可是，俗话说：'每逢佳节倍思亲，'你难道就不想家吗？

陈凯文：当然想，等忙完了这一阵子，我就可以回家了。

王丽莉：那祝你中秋节在学校过得愉快！

陈凯文：也祝你中秋节在家过得愉快！

Answer Questions 回答问题

1. 陈凯文今年回不回家过中秋节？为什么？Is Kevin Chen going home for the Mid-Autumn Festival? Why?
2. 陈凯文家是怎样过中秋节的？How does Kevin Chen's family celebrate the Mid-Autumn Festival?
3. 王丽莉今年回不回家过中秋节？为什么？Is Lily Wang going home for the Mid-Autumn Festival? Why?
4. 王丽莉家是怎样过中秋节的？How does Lily Wang's family celebrate the Mid-Autumn Festival?

Vocabulary 生词

1. 中秋节	zhōngqiūjié	n	Mid-Autumn Festival
2. 功课	gōngkè	n	homework; school work
3. 可能	kěnéng	adv	perhaps
4. 然后	ránhòu	adv	afterward; then
5. 院子	yuànzi	n	yard
6. 赏月	shǎngyuè	v	to admire the moon
7. 少不了	shǎobuliǎo	v	cannot do without
8. 月饼	yuè bǐng	n	moon cake
9. 甜	tián	a	sweet
10. 蛋糕	dàngāo	n	cake
11. 没意思	méiyìsi	a	boring; bored
12. 举办	jǔbàn	v	to hold (an event)
13. 晚会	wǎnhuì	n	party
14. 跳舞	tiàowǔ	v	to dance, dance
15. 可是	kěshì	conj	but

16. 俗话	súhuà	n	old saying
17. 每逢佳节倍思亲	měiféngjiājiébèisīqīn	idiom	one is especially homesick on holidays
18. 难道	nándào	adv	isn't it true
19. 等	děng	v	to wait
20. 一阵子	yízhènzi	adv	a while
21. 愉快	yúkuài	a	happy

Short Reading 阅读短文

　　中秋节是农历八月十五，是中国汉族的四大传统节日之一。关于中秋节，中国有许多传说，如'常娥奔月'、'玉兔捣药'等等，都跟月亮有关。因为中秋节正好是满月，月亮特别圆也特别亮，所以人们喜欢在那天晚上出来赏月，品尝月饼，庆祝全家团圆，祈求生活美满幸福。我觉得中秋节是一个很有趣的节日。

Answer Questions 回答问题

1. 中秋节一般在每年的什么时候？When does the Mid-Autumn Festival fall on in a year?

2. 中秋节对中国汉族人来说有多重要？How important is the Mid-Autumn Festival for Han Chinese?

3. 中秋节的月亮怎么样？为什么？How is the Moon on the Mid-Autumn Festival? Why?

4. 中秋节是庆祝什么的？What does the Mid-Autumn Festival celebrate?

Vocabulary 生词

1. 月	yuè	n	moon; month
2. 之一	zhīyī	pron	one of
3. 关于	guānyú	prep	about
4. 许多	xǔduō	a	many

176

5.	传说	chuánshuō	n	legend
6.	跟...有关		vp	to be related to
7.	月亮	yuèliang	n	moon
8.	因为	yīnwèi	conj	because
9.	满月	mǎnyuè	n	full moon
10.	圆	yuán	a/n	round; circle
11.	亮	liàng	a	bright
12.	所以	suóyǐ	conj	so; therefore
13.	晚上	wǎnshàng	n	evening; night
14.	出来	chūlái	v	to come out
15.	庆祝	qìngzhù	v	to celebrate
16.	祈求	qíqiú	v	to pray for
17.	美满	měimǎn	a	perfect
18.	幸福	xìngfú	a	happy; blessed
19.	有趣	yǒuqù	a	interesting

Proper Nouns 专有名词

1.	汉族	hànzú	the Chinese Han ethnicity
2.	嫦娥奔月	cháng'ébēnyuè	Chang'e Ascending the Moon
3.	玉兔捣药	yùtùdǎoyào	Jade Rabbit Grinding Elixirs

Task 1 Pair Activity 双人活动

Pretend the Mid-Autumn Festival is coming. Ask your partner what his/her plan is for the holiday. Try to persuade your partner to change his/her plan.

Task 2 Group/Class Activity 小组/全班活动

Working in small groups, create a power-point presentation about one legendary story associated with the Mid-Autumn Festival and show it to the whole class. You may choose such stories as 月饼的来历，后羿射日，嫦娥奔月，吴刚伐桂，玉兔捣药, etc.

Character Notes 汉字讲解

1. 点横头

   The 'lid radical' is found in a group of words whose shared properties are unclear now. For example:

亮	liàng	a	bright
离	lí	prep	away from
高	gāo	a	high; tall
夜	yè	n	eve; night
衰	shuāi	v	to deteriate
商	shāng	n	business

2. 日字旁

   The 'sun radical' implies 'the sun.' For example:

晚	wǎn	n/a	evening; late
早	zǎo	n/adj	morning; early
时	shí	n	time
春	chūn	n	spring

3. 虫字旁

   The 'worm radical' implies 'insect' or 'animals that crawl.' For example:

蛋	dàn	n	egg
虾	xiā	n	shrimp

4. 米字旁

   The 'rice radical' implies 'rice.' For example:

糕	gāo	n	cake
粉	fěn	n	flour

Grammar and Usage 语法讲解

1. 还是 'still' can be used in an affirmative sentence to indicate the speaker's preference.
   For example:
   1) 今年中秋我还是想回家过节。This Mid-Autumn Festival I would rather go home to celebrate the holiday.
   2) 我还是更喜欢住在城里。I prefer living in the city.
   3) 比起中秋节来，我还是更喜欢过春节。Compared with Mid-Autumn Festival, I prefer Spring Festival.

2. 难道 'isn't it true' is used in rhetorical questions to express the speaker's doubt or slight disagreement. For example:
   1) 你是中国人，难道连中文都不会说？You are Chinese. Don't you speak Chinese?
   2) 她是学音乐的，难道不会唱歌？She studies music. Isn't it odd that she doesn't know how to sing?

3. 少不了 'with no exception' means that an event routinely occurs. For example:
   1) 中国人过节少不了吃团圆饭。Chinese people cannot do without a family feast for holidays.
   2) 去中国人家做客少不了要脱鞋。When visiting Chinese homes, one always takes off his/her shoes.

4. 因为…所以… 'Because…so…' Unlike in English, cause and effect is expressed in Chinese by pairing 因为 with 所以, placing the cause before the effect.
   For example:
   1) 因为我是中国人，所以我要学中文。Because I am Chinese, (so) I need to learn Chinese language.
   2) 因为我很忙，所以今年中秋我就不回家了。 Because I am very busy, (so) this Autumn Festival I won't be going home.

Cultural Information 文化常识

1. 中秋节 'Mid-Autumn Festival'

The Mid-Autumn Festival, also known as the 'Moon Festival,' is one of the most popular traditional Chinese holidays next to the Lunar New Year. Falling on the fifteenth day of the eighth month of the Lunar calendar (late September to early October in the Solar calendar), it is a festival that celebrates the autumn harvest. On that day, the moon is said to be the fullest and brightest in a year. Chinese people like to eat moon cakes and admire the moon under the moonlight with their family members and friends. It is a time for family reunion as well as a time to pray for happiness. There are many legendary stories that go with the Mid-Autumn Festival, the most famous of which is 'Chang'e Rising to the Moon.' Mid-Autumn Festival is widely celebrated throughout China as well as other Asian countries like Korea, Japan, Vietnam, Singapore, Malaysia, and the Philippines in different forms.

2. 汉族 'the Han ethnicity'

The Han ethnicity is the largest ethnicity in China, comprising approximately 95% of the population. The Han people traced their origin to the Han Dynasty (202 BC- 9 AD). It has the longest uninterrupted history documented and is the largest ethnicity in the world.

3. 嫦娥奔月 'Chang'e asending the Moon', 玉兔捣药 'Jade Rabbit Grinding Elixirs'

One popular Chinese legend has it that Chang'e and her husband Houyi were immortals living in heaven. One day, the ten sons of the Jade Emperor transformed into ten suns, causing the earth to scorch. Having failed to order his sons to stop ruining the earth, the Jade Emperor summoned Houyi for help. Houyi, using his legendary archery skills, shot down nine of the sons, but spared one son to be the sun. The Jade Emperor was obviously not pleased with Houyi's solution to save the earth: nine of his sons were dead. As punishment, the Jade Emperor banished Houyi and Chang'e to live as mere mortals on earth.

Seeing that Chang'e felt extremely miserable over her loss of immortality, Houyi decided to journey on a long, perilous quest to find the pill of immortality so that the couple could be immortals again. At the end of his quest he met the Queen Mother of the West who agreed to give him the pill, but warned him that each person would only need half the pill to become immortal.

Houyi brought the pill home and stored it in a case. He warned Chang'e not to open the case and then left home for a while. Like Pandora in Greek mythology, Chang'e became too curious: she opened up the case and found the pill just as Houyi was returning home. Nervous that Houyi would catch her discovering the contents of the case, she accidentally swallowed the entire pill. She started to float into the sky because of the overdose. Although Houyi wanted to shoot her down in order to prevent her from floating further, he could not bear to aim the arrow at her. Chang'e kept on floating until she landed on the moon.

While she became lonely on the moon without her husband, she did have company. A jade rabbit, who manufactured elixirs, as well as the woodcutter Wu Gang, also lived on the moon.

Pattern Drill 句型操练

Substitute the underlined parts in the following sentences with phrases in the box.

1. <u>今年是我第一年离开家上大学</u>，我还是<u>想回家过中秋</u>。

i. 这个星期我的功课很忙	不要回家过周末了吧
ii. 月饼太甜了	吃蛋糕算了
iii. 这套新款的衣服太贵了	买那套算了
iv. 学校餐厅的菜太不好吃了	自己做菜吧

2. A: <u>俗话说:'每逢佳节倍思亲,'</u> 你难道就不想家吗？

   B：当然想，<u>等忙完了这一阵子，我就可以回家了</u>。

A:		B.	
i. 大家都去中国城喝早茶	跟我们一起去	i. 可是我真的没有时间	
ii. 这是最新的电子游戏	买一个	ii. 可是我没有钱	
iii. 这是现在最流行的歌	唱一唱	iii. 可是我唱得不好听	
iv. 你的厨艺可真好	开一家餐馆	iv. 可是我没有头款	

3. <u>中秋节</u>少不了<u>吃月饼</u>。

i. 中国人过节	吃团圆饭
ii. 农历新年	送红包
iii. 当今的年轻人	上网冲浪
iv. 吃中餐	喝茶

4. 因为<u>中秋节月亮特别圆,特别亮</u>,所以<u>人们喜欢在那天晚上出来赏月</u>。

i.	农历新年是一年的第一天	中国人在那天要穿(chuān, wear)新衣新鞋
ii.	过节全家人都回来了	家里非常热闹
iii.	网上的信息应有尽有	上网冲浪是最快最方便的
iv.	电子游戏很好玩	很多年轻人迷上了电子游戏

Exercises 练习

1. Write the Chinese characters that correspond to the following words in *pinyin.*

   1)tiàowǔ   3) yúkuài   5)qíqiú   7)xìngfú   9)měimǎn

   2)líkāi   4)yǒuqù   6)gōngkè   8)nándào   10)qìngzhù

2. Match the words on the top line with words that typically go with them on the bottom line.

   祈求   品尝   举办   庆祝   美满

   生活   晚会   幸福   月饼   节日

3. Guess the meaning and sound of the following characters by breaking them down to their respective semantic and phonetic parts.

   1) 亡 = _____ + _____ sound: _____ meaning: _____

   2) 明 = _____ + _____ sound: _____ meaning: _____

   3) 蚂 = _____ + _____ sound: _____ meaning: _____

   4) 粒 = _____ + _____ sound: _____ meaning: _____

4. Form two compound words with the characters given and then make a sentence for each of the words.

1) 月 _____ _____

_____ _____

2) 节 _____ _____

_____ _____

3) 尝 _____ _____

_____ _____

4) 快 _____ _____

_____ _____

5. Fill in the blanks in the following passage with the words given; you may use the same words more than once.

最   一边   也   就   除了...以外   了

小的时候，_____农历新年_____，我_____喜欢过中秋节。

中秋节的晚上，月亮特别地圆，_____特别地亮。我们全家人吃完

晚饭以后，_____坐在院子里，_____品尝月饼、_____赏月，

非常有趣。

6. Translate the following sentences into Chinese.

1) Mid-Autumn Festival is one of the four most important Han Chinese holidays.
2) One is especially homesick during holidays.
3) Because I am particularly busy lately, (so) I am not going home this weekend.
4) Chinese cannot do without eating moon cakes on Mid-Autumn Festival.
5) Between Lunar New Year and Mid-Autumn Festival, I would rather celebrate Lunar New Year.
6) Almost everyone has heard of legends related to the moon.
7) Haven't you heard of the legend of "Chang'e Asending the Moon?"
8) Wishing you a happy Mid-Autumn Festival!

7. Write a paragraph about 75-100 characters about how your family celebrates the Mid-Autumn Festival.

Character Stroke Order 生字笔画

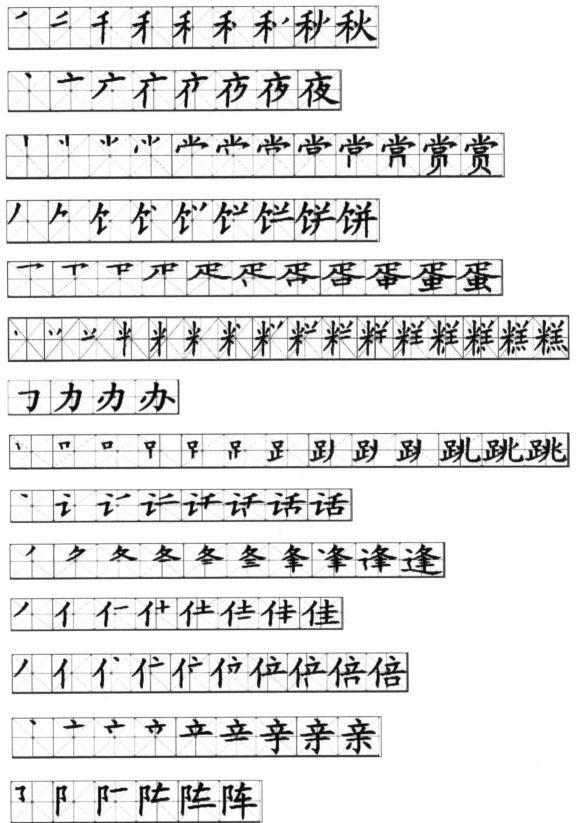

丿 二 千 禾 禾 禾 利 秋 秋

丶 亠 广 疒 疒 夜 夜 夜

丨 丨 丷 丷 当 当 常 常 常 赏 赏

丿 勹 勹 饣 饣 饼 饼 饼 饼

一 厂 厂 正 正 正 疋 番 番 蛋 蛋 蛋

丶 丷 丷 半 米 米 米 料 料 料 粒 糕 糕 糕

丁 力 办 办

丨 叮 口 甲 甲 足 足 趴 趴 趴 跳 跳 跳

丶 讠 讠 讠 讠 讠 话 话

丿 夕 冬 冬 冬 备 夆 逢 逢

丿 亻 仁 什 件 佳 佳 佳

丿 亻 亻 亻 仕 位 位 倍 倍 倍

丶 亠 亠 立 立 辛 辛 亲

了 阝 阝 阵 阵 阵

184

、 ｜ 忄 忄 忄 忄 忄 恰 愉 愉 愉

、 讠 讠 许 许 许

丶 十 亠 市 古 声 声 亮

丶 亠 广 庐 庆 庆

丶 ゝ ネ ネ 礻 祈 祈 祈

一 寸 寸 才 求 求 求

丶 ⺌ 丷 半 半 羊 美 美

一 十 士 丰 丰 击 幸 幸

一 十 土 キ 丰 赤 走 走 起 起 趄 趄 趄 趣 趣

了 阝 阝 阝 阼 陀 陀 院 院

丿 二 千 千 舌 舌 舌 甜 甜 甜 甜

丶 丷 ⺍ 丷 兴 兴 兴 举 举

丶 冫 氵 汀 汉

丶 二 亍 方 方 扩 扩 斿 斿 族

185

Unit Seven 第七单元

Chinese Americans 美籍华人

Source: mrthompson.org

Lesson 13 第十三课 My Double Identity 我的双重身份

Think and Share 想想说说

1. 你是在哪里出生、哪里长大的？Where were you born? Where did you grow up?
2. 你喜欢吃中国餐还是美国餐？Do you prefer Chinese food or American food?
3. 你过不过中国的传统节日？Do you celebrate Chinese traditional holidays?
4. 你觉得自己是中国人还是美国人？为什么？Do you consider yourself Chinese or American? Why?

Dialogue 对话

陈凯文：那天我跟几个中国同学讨论一个问题，就是，我们到底是中国人还是美国人。

王丽莉：你觉得自己是中国人还是美国人呢？

陈凯文：我觉得自己是中国人，因为我长着黄皮肤、黑眼睛、黑头发，是中国人的后代。

王丽莉：就这些吗？

陈凯文：不光是这些。还有，我在家讲的是中国话，吃的是中国饭，朋友也大多是中国人。

王丽莉：你讲的有道理。不过，我还是觉得自己是美国人。

陈凯文：为什么？

王丽莉：因为我是在美国出生、美国长大的，从来没有去过中国，朋友也大多是美国人。

陈凯文：就这些吗？

王丽莉：不光是这些。还有，我平时讲的是英文，听的是美国流行音乐，吃的是美式快餐。

陈凯文：但是你过不过中国传统节日呀？

王丽莉：中国节日、美国节日，我都过。

陈凯文：看来你既是中国人，又是美国人。

王丽莉：是呀，所以我们应该都是美籍华人。

Answer Questions 回答问题

1. 陈凯文觉得自己是中国人还是美国人？为什么？Does Kevin Chen consider himself Chinese or American? Why?
2. 王丽莉觉得自己是中国人还是美国人？为什么？Does Lily Wang consider herself Chinese or American? Why？
3. 为什么说他们应该都是美籍华人？Why it is better to call them 'Chinese Americans'?

Vocabulary 生词

1.	那天	nàtiān	pron	the other day; that day
2.	同学	tóngxué	n	classmate, schoolmate
3.	讨论	tǎolùn	v/n	to discuss; discussion
4.	到底	dàodǐ	adv	afterall
5.	长	zhǎng	v	to grow
6.	黄	huáng	a	yellow
7.	皮肤	pífū	n	skin
8.	黑	hēi	a	black
9.	眼睛	yǎnjing	n	eye
10.	头发	tóufà	n	hair
11.	后代	hòudài	n	offspring
12.	这些	zhèxiē	pron	these
13.	不光	bùguāng	conj/adv	not just; not only
14.	中国话	zhōngguóhuà	n	spoken Chinese
15.	讲	jiǎng	v	to speak

16. 话	huà	n	spoken language; speech
17. 大多	dàduō	adv	mostly
18. 道理	dàolǐ	n	reason
19. 出生	chūshēng	v	to be born
20. 长大	zhǎngdà	v	to grow up
21. 从来	cónglái	adv	ever
22. 平时	píngshí	adv	usually
23. 英文	yīngwén	n	English language
24. 美式	měishì	a	American style
25. 快餐	kuàicān	n	fast food
26. 看来	kànlái	v	it seems; it looks; it appears
27. 既...又...	jì…yòu…	conj	both...and…
28. 美籍华人	měijíhuárén	n	Chinese American

Short Reading 阅读短文

我们这些在美国出生、美国长大的中国人，大多都会面临这么一个问题：自己到底是中国人还是美国人。在面孔和家教方面，更像中国人；但是，在许多生活习惯和兴趣爱好方面，又更像美国人。因此，我们是有着双重身份的人，即美籍华人。

Answer Questions 回答问题

1. 在美国出生的中国人一般都面临着一个什么问题？Which question do most American-born Chinese face?
2. 在哪些方面他们更像中国人？In which areas do they resemble Chinese?
3. 在哪些方面他们更像美国人？In which areas do they resemble Americans?
4. 那些有中美双重身份的人叫着什么？What is the term for people who have both Chinese and American identities?

Vocabulary 生词

1.	面临	miànlín	v	to face
2.	面孔	miànkǒng	n	face; looks
3.	家教	jiājiào	n	upbring
4.	方面	fāngmiàn	n	area, aspect
5.	兴趣	xìngqù	n	interest
6.	爱好	àihào	n	hobby
7.	因此	yīncǐ	conj	therefore
8.	双重	shuāngchóng	a	double
9.	身份	shēnfèn	n	identity
10.	即	jí	conj	hence

Task 1 Pair Activity/Group 双人/小组活动

Talk with your classmates about your perception of your cultural identity over time. When you were little, did you consider yourself Chinese or American? How about now? If different, what has changed your perception? Compare your answers with those of your partner's.

Task 2 Group Activity 小组活动

In a small group, compare and contrast how Chinese and American families raise their children. In what ways are they similar and in what ways are they different? Which way do you prefer and why?

Character Notes 汉字讲解

1. 夕字旁

   The 'sunset radical' implies 'evening.' For example:

多	duō	a	many; much
外	wài	a	outside
岁	suì	n	years of age
夜	yè	n	eve; night

190

| 名 | míng | n | name |
| 舞 | wǔ | n | dance |

2. 大字旁

The 'big radical' implies 'big.' For example:

美	měi	a	beautiful
太	tài	adv	too
头	tóu	n	head
买	mǎi	v	to buy

3. 子字旁

The 'son radical' implies 'son.' For example:

孔	kǒng	n	hole
学	xué	v	to study
孙	sūn	n	grandson

4. 广字旁

The 'wide radical' implies 'spaciousness' or 'building.' For example:

底	dǐ	n	bottom
座	zuò	m	(measure for twon or building)
店	diàn	n	shop; store

Grammar 语法讲解

1. 到底 'afterall' is used in a question for emphasis. For example:

   1) 我们到底是中国人还是美国人？Are we ultimately Chinese or American?
   2) 你到底想吃中餐还是吃西餐？What do you really want to eat---Chinese or Western food?
   3) 你到底上哪里去了？Where on earth did you go?

2. 既…又… 'both…and…' is a parallel conjunction used to combine verbs, adjectives, or adverbs. For example:

   1) 我们既是中国人，又是美国人。We are both Chinese and American.
   2) 我们的校园既大又美丽。Our campus is both large and beautiful.
   3) 他的中文说得既快又好。 He speaks Chinese both fast and well.

191

3. 在…方面 is a prepositional phrase with a noun phrase in the middle to indicate 'in the area of'. For example:

1) 在家教方面我们像中国人，可是在兴趣方面我们更像美国人。In terms of family upbrings, we are more like Chinese, but in terms of interests, we are more like Americans.
2) 王丽莉在音乐方面很有兴趣，陈凯文在游戏机方面很有研究。Lily Wang is very interested in the area of music; Kevin Chen is very knowledgeable in the aspect of video games.
3) 美籍华人在科学技术方面有着很大成就。Chinese Americans have great accomplishments in science and technology.

4. 即是 is a formal expression that means 'that is'. For example：

1) 我们都是有双重身份的人，即是美籍华人。We are all people of dual identities, that is, Chinese Americans.
2) 唐人街，即是中国城，是华人聚集的地方。Tangren Street, that is 'Chinatown', is a place where Chinese gather.
3) 通俗音乐即是流行音乐。Pop music is popular music.

Pattern Drill 句型操练

Substitute the underlined parts in the following sentences with phrases in the box.

1. A: 看来你既是中国人，又是美国人。

   B: 是呀，我们应该都是美籍华人。

A. i. 你吃不惯美国餐	B. i. 我是地地道道(dìdidàodào, out-and-out)的中国人
ii. 玩电子游戏会影响功课	ii. 我经常玩到很晚，第二天上课直打瞌睡
iii. 你喜欢逛商场	iii. 我差不多一有时间就去逛街
iv. 你不喜欢你的大学生活	iv. 每天除了上课，就是自习，没有意思

2. 在许多生活习惯和兴趣爱好方面，我们更像美国人。

i.	饮食(yǐnshí, eating)习惯	我更像一个中国人
ii.	举止 (jǔzhǐ, mannerism)	我更像一个美国人
iii.	文化传统	中国有着很长的历史
iv.	高科技	美国比较发达(fādá, advanced)

3. A: 我们到底是中国人还是美国人？

   B: 我们即是中国人，又是美国人。

A. i.	你	想	不想跟我们一起去KTV
B. i.	我	想去	不想去
A. ii.	他	喜欢古典音乐	喜欢流行音乐
B. ii.	他	喜欢古典音乐	喜欢流行音乐
A. iii.	你们	想吃中餐	想吃西餐
B. iii.	我们	想吃中餐	想吃西餐
A. iv.	你	要买衣服	要买电子游戏
B. iv.	我	要买衣服	要买电子游戏

Exercises 练习

1. Write the Chinese characters that correspond to the words in *pinyin*.

   1) juéde   3)dàolǐ   5) kuàicān   7) xìngqù   9) miànlín

   2) wèntí   4)shuāngchóng   6) miànkǒng   8) měijí   10) hēiyǎnjing

2. Match the words on the top line with words that typically go with them on the bottom line.

讨论　　　　　生活　　　双重　　　　兴趣　　　　美籍

习惯　　　　　华人　　　爱好　　　　问题　　　　身份

3. Guess the meaning and sound of the following characters by breaking them down to their respective semantic and phonetic parts.

1) 梦 = _____ + _____ sound: _____ meaning: _____

2) 卖 = _____ + _____ sound: _____ meaning: _____

3) 李 = _____ + _____ sound: _____ meaning: _____

4) 床 = _____ + _____ sound: _____ meaning: _____

4. Form two compound words with the characters given and write a sentence by using each of the compound words.

1) 生　_____　_____

　　　　_____　_____

2) 兴　_____　_____

　　　　_____　_____

3) 华　_____　_____

　　　　_____　_____

4) 面　_____　_____

　　　　_____　_____

194

5. Fill in the blanks with the words given, one for each blank.

在…方面　　　既…又　　　　　即是　　　到底　　　还是

我们这些在美国长大的中国人，经常问自己一个问题，_____，

"我们_____是中国人_____美国人？"_____语言_____，

我们_____会讲中文_____会讲英文，我们应该都是美籍华人。

6. Translate the following sentences into Chinese.

   1) I am an American-born and American-raised Chinese.
   2) In terms of food (饮食), I am more like a Chinese.
   3) In terms of hobby, I am more like an American.
   4) I look like Chinese in appearance, but I am more like American in mannerism (举止).
   5) I am both Chinese and American.

7. Write a short composition (approximately100 words) about your perception of yourself in terms of ethnic identity. Explain what has influenced your perception of your ethnic identity.

Character Stroke Order 生字笔画

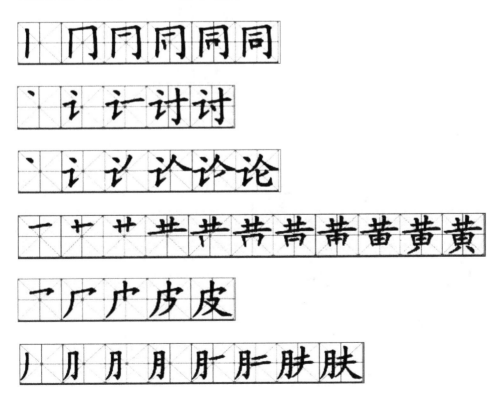

黑　丨　冂　冋　四　四　甲　甼　里　黒　黑　黑　黑

眼　丨　冂　冂　月　目　目ˋ　目ˊ　目ˋ　眼　眼　眼

睛　丨　冂　冂　月　目　目ˋ　目ˊ　目ˋ　睛　睛　睛　睛

些　丨　上　止　此　此　此　此　些

平　一　一　一　平　平

既　ㄱ　ㄱ　ㄹ　ㄹ　目　目　目ˊ　既　既

籍　丿　ㄏ　ㅅ　ㅆ　竹　竹　笶　笐　笋　笋　笋　筚　笋　籍　籍　籍　籍

面　一　一　一　丙　而　而　而　面　面

临　丨　刂　ㄓ　忙　忙　忙　临　临　临

孔　ㄱ　了　子　孔

更　一　一　一　而　而　更　更

此　丨　上　止　此　此　此

双　ㄱ　又　双　双

196

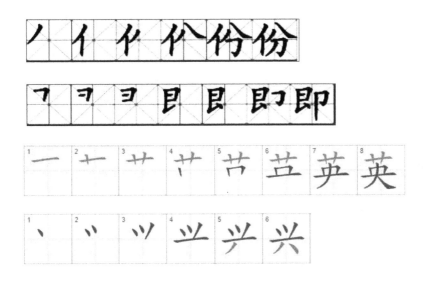

1	2	3	4	5	6	7	8
一	十	艹	芓	节	苎	英	英

1	2	3	4	5	6
丶	丷	丷	兴	兴	兴

Lesson 14 第十四课 Chinese in America 华人在美

Think and Share 想想说说

1. 你知道华人最早是什么时候来美国的吗？Do you know when the earliest Chinese immigrants came to the United States?
2. 早期的华人大多数是从事什么工作的？为什么？What occupations were most early Chinese immigrants employed in? Why?
3. 他们在美国的待遇怎么样？How were they treated in the U.S.?
4. 一九六五年后的华人移民在美国的待遇又怎么样？How do post-1965 Chinese immigrants fare in the U.S.?

Dialogue 对话

王丽莉：今天我学习了华人在美国的历史。你知道华人最早是什么时候来美国的吗？

陈凯文：是不是十九世纪初期？

王丽莉：是的，最早的华人是 1820 年移民来美国的。不过，1848 年加州淘金热以后，才有大批的华人移民来美国。

陈凯文：早期华人移民来美国都是做什么工作的？

王丽莉：早期移民来美国的华人大多是男劳工，从事金矿、铁路、餐馆、洗衣店等工作。

陈凯文：那他们一定受到了不少歧视。

王丽莉：是的。他们大多没受过什么教育，被当成"苦力"。1884 到 1943 年期间，美国政府禁止华人移民。

陈凯文：那到什么时候华人又可以大批地移民来美国了呢？

王丽莉：那是 1965 年以后，随着移民法的修改，大批的华人涌入了美国。近期华人移民在美国从事各行各业的工作，有工程师、医生、商人、还有国家公务员等等。

Answer Questions 回答问题

1. 早期华人是什么时候大批地移民来美国的？When was the earliest wave of Chinese immigrants to the U.S.?
2. 什么期间美国政府禁止华人移民来美国？Which period of time did the U.S. government prohibit Chinese from immigrating to the U.S.?
3. 什么时候华人又可以大批地移民来美国了？When were Chinese allowed to immigrate to the U.S. in large numbers?
4. 近期华人在美国都是从事什么工作的？Which occupations are recent immigrants from China employed in?

Vocabulary 生词

1. 今天	jīntiān	n	today
2. 学习	xuéxí	v/n	to study; study
3. 知道	zhīdào	v	to know
4. 世纪	shìjì	n	century
5. 初期	chūqī	n	early period
6. 以后	yǐhòu	prep	after
7. 大批	dàpī	a/adv	large number of; in large numbers
8. 早期	zǎoqī	a	early
9. 大多	dàduō	adv	mostly
10. 男	nán	a	male
11. 劳工	láogōng	n	laborer
12. 从事	cóngshì	v	to be engaged in (line of work)
13. 金矿	jīnkuàng	n	gold mine
14. 铁路	tiělù	n	railroad
15. 受(到)	shòudào	v	to be subjected to; to receive
16. 歧视	qíshì	n	discrimination

17. 教育	jiàoyù	n	education
18. 当成	dāng chéng	v	to treat as
19. 苦力	kǔlì	n	hard laborer
20. 期间	qījiān	n	period of time
21. 政府	zhèngfǔ	n	govement
22. 禁止	jìnzhǐ	v	to prohibit
23. 移民法	yímínfǎ	n	immigration law
24. 修改	xiūgǎi	v/n	to revise; amendment
25. 涌入	yǒngrù	v/n	to pour in; influx
26. 近期	jìnqī	n	recent time
27. 各行各业	gèhánggèyè	idiom	all walks of life
28. 医生	yīshēng	n	doctor
29. 商人	shāngrén	n	business person
30. 公务员	gōngwùyuán	n	public servant

Proper Nouns 专有名词

1. 加州	jiāzhōu	California
2. 淘金热	táojīnrè	Gold Rush

Short Reading 阅读短文

　　华人移民来美国已经有190多年的历史了。早期的移民大多来自于广东，他们从事各种体力劳动，如采矿、修铁路、打餐馆、开洗衣店等等，受到了许多歧视。近期的移民先是来自于香港、台湾，后是来自于中国内地。除了从事传统的工作以外，他们还在各行各业取得了巨大的成就。

Answer Questions 回答问题

1. 华人移民来美有多长时间的历史了？How long is the history of Chinese immigration to the United States?
2. 早期华人移民主要是来自于哪里？Where did early Chinese immigrants mostly come from?
3. 早期华裔移民在美国大多从事什么工作？Which line of work were early Chinese immigrants engaged in?
4. 近期华裔移民在美国的情况怎么样？How about Chinese immigrants in recent years?

Vocabulary 生词

1. 体力	tǐlì	a/n	physical; manual
2. 劳动	láodòng	n/v	labor
3. 采矿	cǎikuàng	v	to mine
4. 修	xiū	v	to build, to fix
5. 许多	xǔduō	a	many; a lot of
6. 后	hòu	adv	later
7. 内地	nèidì	n	inland
8. 取得	qǔdé	v	to achieve
9. 巨大	jùdà	a	great
10. 成就	chéngjiù	n	accomplishment

Task 1 Pair Activity 双人活动

Pretend to be a news reporter interviewing a famous Chinese American played by your partner about his/her success story. You may optionally perform this skit for the whole class.

Task 2 Class Activity 全班活动

Watch a movie or documentary such as Becoming American about Chinese immigrants in the United States.

Character Notes 汉字讲解

1. 爪字旁

   The 'claw radical' implies 'claw' or actions involving hands. For example:

受	shou	v	to receive
爱	ài	v	to love
采	cǎi	v	to mine
彩	cǎi	n	color
菜	cài	n	vegetable

2. 止字旁

   The 'stop radical' implies 'to stop.' For example:

止	zhǐ	v	to stop
歧	qì	v	to diccriminate
此	cǐ	pron	this
些	xiē	a	some

3. 之字旁

   The 'go radical' implies 'to go.' For example:

各	gè	a	every
务	wù	n	service
条	tiáo	m	(thin, long strip)
备	bèi	v	to prepare

4. 戈字旁

   The 'dagger radical' implies 'weapon' or 'war.' For example:

成	chéng	v	to become
我	wǒ	pron	I, me
或	huò	conj	or

Grammar and Usage 语法讲解

1. 先…后… 'first…then…' is used to sequence the order of events. For example:

   1) 近期移民先是来自香港、台湾，后是来自中国内地。Recent immigrants first

came from Hong Kong and Taiwan, later from Mainland China.

2) 喝茶的时候，先点茶，后点点心。When having morning tea, first order tea, then Dim Sum.

3) 我们先上大学，后找工作。We first go to college and then look for a job.

2. 190 多年 means 'one hundred and ninety some years". When 多 is added to a number, it indicates that the number is an estimate, not a precise number. For example,

1）她看上去有二十多岁。She looks like she is in her 20s.

2）从学校到中国城开车要两个多小时。It takes over two hours to get to Chinatown from school.

3）我收到了一百多块钱的红包。I received over one hundred some dollars in red envelopes.

Pattern Drill 句型操练

1. A: <u>他们一定受到了不少歧视</u>。

B: 是的。<u>他们大多没受过什么教育，被当成'苦力'</u>。

A. i. 你　　是在美国出生、美国长大的中国人

B. i. 我是地地道道的美籍华人

A. ii. 老师　很了解 (liǎojiě, familiar with)华人在美的历史

B. ii. 她是主修亚 (yà, Asian)美研究专业的

A. iii. 你们　会面临这个问题

B. iii. 我们是有着双重身份的人

A. iv. 你　　很想家

B. iv. 今年是我第一年上大学

---

2. <u>近期的移民先是来自于香港、台湾，后是来自于中国内地。</u>

i. 我的父母	从广东移民到香港	从香港移民到美国
ii. 中秋夜我家	吃一顿团圆饭	到院子里赏月
iii. 大年初一我们	给长辈拜年	去中国城看舞狮
iv. 新年前大家	先打扫房间	购买年货

Exercises 练习

1. Write the Chinese characters corresponding to the words in *pinyin*.

    1) cóngshì   3) chéngjiù   5) suízhe   7) zhèngfǔ   9) qíshì

    2) shòudào   4)gōngwùyuán   6) xiūgǎi   8) jìnzhǐ   10) qǔdé

2. Match the words on the top line with words that typically go with them on the bottom line.

    受到   取得   从事   禁止   来自

    各地   歧视   移民   工作   成就

3. Guess the meaning and sound of the following characters by breaking them down to their respective semantic and phonetic parts.

    1) 爬 = _____ + _____ sound: _____ meaning: _____

    2) 步 = _____ + _____ sound: _____ meaning: _____

    3) 冬= _____ + _____ sound: _____ meaning: _____

    4) 战= _____ + _____ sound: _____ meaning: _____

204

4. Form two compound words with the character given and make a sentence using each word.

   1) 期　　_____　　_____

   _____　　_____

   2) 各　　_____　　_____

   _____　　_____

   3) 修　　_____　　_____

   _____　　_____

   4) 劳　　_____　　_____

   _____　　_____

5. Fill in the blanks with the words given.

   大多　　　　　　以后　　　　虽然　　　　但是　　　　才　　　　　已经

   _____华人在美_____有近两百年的历史了，_____早

   期华人_____是男劳工，从事淘金和修铁路等体力劳动，受到了许多歧视。

   一九六五年移民法修改_____，华人_____大量地涌入美国，从事各

   行各业的工作，取得了巨大的成就。

6. Translate the following sentences into Chinese.

   1) Chinese already has a long history in the United States.
   2) Early Chinese immigrants mainly worked in physical labor.
   3) They were subjected to a lot of discrimination.
   4) Recent Chinese immigrants are employed in all walks of life in the U.S.
   5) They have achieved great accomplishments.

7. Interview your parent(s) or an older relative in Chinese about their immigrant experience in the United States. Summarize the results of the interview in a paragraph over 100 characters.

8. Search online about a famous Chinese American. Be prepared to report your findings to the class.

丿 と と 乍 矢 知 知 知

一 十 廿 廿 世

乚 幺 纟 纠 纠 纪

丶 丷 氵 汀 汋 沟 沟 沟 淘 淘 淘

丿 人 仐 仐 仐 仐 佥 金

一 寸 才 扌 扎 批 批

丨 冂 日 用 田 甼 男

一 十 艹 芐 芅 劳 劳

一 厂 丆 石 石 矿 矿 矿

丨 上 止 止 此 此 此 歧 歧

一 十 艹 芇 芊 芊 苦 苦

Glossary Index

A

爱	ài	v	to love	L3
爱好	àihào	n	hobby	L13
安静	ānjìng	adj	quiet	L5
安全	ānquán	adj	safe	L5

B

吧	ba	part	(to solicit agreement)	L1
爸爸	bàba	n	dad	L2
巴士	bāshì	n	bus	L5
拜年	bàinián	v	to wish happy new year	L11
半	bàn	adj	half	L5
办	bàn	v	to hold (an event)	L12
帮	bāng	v	to help	L8
包	bāo	v/n	to wrap; parcel	L11
杯	bēi	n/m	cup; (measure for liquid)	L7
被	bèi	co-v	by	L9
比较	bǐjiào	adv	rather; relatively	L5
毕业	bìyè	v	to graduate	L3
鞭炮	biānpàon	n	firecrackers	L11
伯父	bófù	n	uncle (father's older brother); friend's father	L8
伯母	bómǔ	n	aunt (father's older brother's wife); friend's mother	L8
不	bù	adv	no; not	L4
不光	bùguāng	adv	not just; not only	L13
不过	búguò	conj	but	L5
不仅...而且...	bùjǐn...érqiě...	conj	not only...but also	L9
不少	bùshǎo	adj	quite a few	L7
不一定	bùyīdìng	idiom	It depends	L5

C

才	cái	adv	only then	L8
菜单	càidān	n	menu	L7
菜市场	càishìchǎng	n	vegetable stands; farmer's market	L6
采矿	cǎikuàng	v	to mine	L14
餐馆	cānguǎn	n	restaurant	L2
餐厅	cāntīng	n	cafeteria	L3
参加	cānjiā	v	to join; to participate	L4
草坪	cǎopíng	n	lawn	L3
层	céng	m	story (of a building); layer	L8
茶	chá	n	tea	L7
茶叶	cháyè	n	dried tea leaves	L8
差不多	chàbùduō	adv	almost	L10

差点	chàdiǎn	adv	nearly	L4
产品	chǎnpǐn	n	product	L10
尝	cháng	v	to taste	L7
长处	chángchu	n	strength	L9
唱歌	chànggē	v	to sing	L3
吵闹	chǎonào	adj	noisy	L6
超市	chāoshì	n	supermarket	L5
炒	chǎo	v	to stir-fry	L7
称	chēng	v	to be known as	L10
成	chéng	v	to become	L9
成就	chéngjiù	n	accomplishment	L14
城里	chéngli	n	inner city	L5
吃	chī	v	to eat	L4
冲浪	chōnglàng	v	to surf	L10
出来	chūlái	v	to come out	L12
出生	chūshēng	v	to be born	L13
初期	chūqī	n	early period	L14
除了...以外	chúle... yǐwài	prep	except; besides	L3
除夕	chúxī	n	eve	L11
厨房	chúfáng	n	kitchen	L8
厨艺	chuyì	n	culinary art	L8
传说	chuánshuō	n	legend	L12
传统	chuántǒng	a/n	traditional; tradition	L11
春节	chūnjié	n	spring festival; Chinese lunar new year	L11
次	cì	m	(measure word for 'time')	L7
从	cóng	prep	from	L2
从来	cónglái	adv	ever	L13
从事	cóngshì	v	to pursue a career in; to work in	L14
存	cún	v	to deposit	L11
存下来	cúnxiàlái	v	to save up	L11

D

打	dǎ	v	to play (balls); to hit; to wrok	L3
打瞌睡	dǎkēshuì	v	to feel drowsy; to doze off	L10
打扫	dǎsǎo	v	to sweep and dust	L11
打算	dǎsuan	v	to plan	L11
大	dà	a	big, large	L3
大多	dàduō	adv	mostly	L13
大道	dàdào	n	avenue	L5
大二	dàèr	n	(colloq) college sophomore year	L1
大家	dàjiā	n	everybody	L1
大脑	dànǎo	n	brain	L10
大年	dànián	n	New Year	L11
初一	chūyī	n	first day of the month/year	L11
大批	dàpī	a/adv	large number of; in large numbers	L14

大厦	dàshà	n	high rise	L6
大学	dàxué	n	college; university	L1
大学城	dàxuéchéng	n	college town	L3
大一	dàyī	n	(colloq) college freshman year	L1
带	dài	v	to bring	L8
蛋糕	dàngāo	n	cake	L12
但是	dànshì	conj	but	L5
当成	dàngchéng	v	to treat as	L14
当今	dāngjīn	adv	at the present time; nowadays	L9
当然	dāngrán	adv	of course	L5
到	dào	v /prep	to arrive; to reach; to; (resultative complement meaning 'be able to')	L2
到处	dàochù	pron	everywhere	L3
到底	dàodǐ	adv	afterall	L13
道	dào	n/m	course; (measure word for dish)	L8
道理	dàolǐ	n	reason	L13
倒是	dàoshì	adv	(colloq) ironically	L11
的	de	part	(to indicate possession, modification, or to soften speech)	L1
得	de	part	(to introduce a complement)	L2
等	děng	v	to wait	L12
等等	děngděng	part	and so on; and so forth; etc.	L3
第	dì		(prefix for ordinal number)	L10
弟弟	dìdi	n	younger brother	L2
地方	dìfāng	adj/n	local; place	L8
地铁	dìtiě	n	subway	L5
点	diǎn	v	to order (food)	L7
点心	diǎnxin	n	dumplings; dim sum	L7
电脑	diànnǎo	n	computer	L2
电视	diànshì	n	television	L10
电子	diànzǐ	a	electronic	L10
电子游戏	diànzǐyóuxì	n	video games	L3
碟	dié	n/m	plate; (measure word for dish)	L7
东西	dōngxī	n	thing; stuff	L2
动筷	dòngkuài	v	to start eating	L8
动听	dòngtīng	adj	melodious	L9
都	dōu	adv	all; both	L2
锻炼	duànliàn	v/n	to exercise; exercise	L10
对	duì	a/prep	correct; to	L1
对了	duìle	int	oh yes	L4
对不起	duìbùqǐ	idiom	sorry; excuse me	L7
顿	dùn	me	(measure word for meal)	L11
多	duō	adj	many; much	L2

E

而已	éryǐ	adv	that's all	L8

F

发展	fāzhǎn	v/n	to develop; development	L9
饭菜	fàncài	n	food; meal	L4
方便	fāngbiàn	adj/n	convenient; convenience	L5
方面	fāngmiàn	n	area, aspect	L13
方式	fāngshì	n	method	L10
房间	fángjiān	n	room	L11
放	fàng	v	to set off; to place	L11
放松	fàngsōng	v/a	to relax; relaxed	L10
费	fèi	n	fee	L5
非常	fēicháng	adv	extremely	L9
分	fēn	v	to distribute	L11
分钟	fēnzhōng	n	minute	L5
服务员	fúwùyuán	n	waiter; waitress	L7
附近	fùjìn	n/adj	nearby	L5
父母	fùmǔ	n	parent	L2

G

赶	gǎn	v	to rush	L11
刚	gāng	adv	just about	L8
钢琴	gāngqín	n	piano	L3
高	gāo	a	high; tall	L10
高兴	gāoxìng	a	glad	L1
哥哥	gēge	n	older brother	L2
歌曲	gēqǔ	n	song	L9
歌手	gēshǒu	n	singer	L9
个	gè	m	(generic measure word)	L3
各行各业	gèhánggèyè	idiom	all walks of life	L14
各式各样	gèshìgèyàng	idiom	all kinds of	L7
各种	gèzhǒng	a	all kinds of	L14
给	gěi	v	to give	L8
跟	gēn	prep	with	L2
更	gèng	adv	even more	L10
工程师	gōngchéngshī	n	engineer	L2
工作	gōngzuò	n	job	L2
功课	gōngkè	n	homework; school work	L12
公司	gōngsī	n	company	L11
公务员	gōngwùyuán	n	public servant	L14
公园	gōngyuán	n	park	L5
恭喜发财	gōngxǐfācái	idiom	wishing you a prosperous new year	L11
够	gòu	adv	enough	L11
购买	gòumǎi	v	to purchase	L11

购物	gòuwù	n/v	to shop; shopping	L10
古典	gǔdiǎn	adj	classical	L9
关	guān	v	to close	L8
关于	guānyú	prep	about	L12
光	guāng	a/n	used up (used after a verb as a resultative complement); light	L4
管理	guǎnlǐ	v/n	to manage; management	L2
逛	guàng	v	to stroll; to wander	L10
贵	guì	adj	expensive	L5
国家	guójiā	n	country; nation	L6
过	guò	v/part	to pass; (experiential particle); to observe holiday	L6
过年	guònián	v	to celebrate new year	L11

H

嗨	hāi	Int	hi	L1
还	hái	adv	still, also	L2
还好	háihǎo	idiom	it's alright	L4
还有	háiyǒu	conj	also	L3
好	hǎo	a/adv	good; well	L1
好吃	hǎochī	adj	delicious	L4
好像	hǎoxiàng	prep	like; such as	L10
号	hào	n	number	L6
喝	hē	v	to drink	L7
和	hé	conj	and	L2
黑	hēi	a	black	L13
很	hěn	adv	very	L1
红	hóng	adj	red	L7
红包	hóngbāo	n	red envelope	L11
猴	hóu	n	monkey	L1
后	hòu	adv	later	L14
后代	hòudài	n	offspring	L13
后来	hòulái	adv	later	L9
花	huā	v/n	to spend; flower	L4
互联网	hùliánwǎng	n	internet	L10
护士	hùshi	n	nurse	L2
华裔	huáyì	adj	of Chinese descent	L6
化学	huàxué	n	chemistry	L3
欢迎	huānyíng	v/n	to welcome; welcome	L5
欢迎光临	huānyíngguānglín	(idiom)	welcome (formal)	L7
换上	huànshàng	v	to change into	L8
黄	huáng	a	yellow	L13
会	huì	aux	will; know how	L4
回家	huíjiā	v	to go home	L11
活动	huódòng	n	activity	L3

获取	huòqǔ	v	to obtain	L10
或者	huòzhě	conj	or	L6

J

极	jí	adv	extremely	L11
几	jǐ	nu	how many; several	L2
既…又…	jì…yòu…	conj	both...and...	L13
即	jí	conj	hence	L13
家	jiā	n/m	family; home; (measure word for family-run business)	L2
家常便饭	jiāchángbiànfàn		homemade cooking	L8
家教	jiājiào	n	upbring	L13
家人	jiārén	n	family member	L11
夹菜	jiácài	v	to add food with chopsticks	L8
健身房	jiànshēnfáng	n	fitness room	L3
讲	jiǎng	v	to speak	L13
交	jiāo	v	to make acquaintance with; to make friends with	L4
交叉	jiāochā	n/adj	cross; crossed	L5
路口	lùkǒu	n	intersection; block	L5
交流	jiāoliú	v	to exchange	L1
交通	jiāotōng	n	traffic; transportation	L5
饺子	jiǎozi	n	Chinese dumplings	L11
叫	jiào	v	to be called by the name of	L1
教室	jiàoshì	n	classroom	L4
教堂	jiàotáng	n	church	L6
教学楼	jiàoxuélóu	n	classroom building	L3
教育	jiàoyù	n	education	L14
街	jiē	n	street	L5
街区	jiēqū	n	neighborhood; block	L5
街心	jiēxīn	n	street corner	L6
接受	jiēshòu	v	to receiv; to accept	L9
结合	jiéhé	v	to combine	L9
节日	jiérì	n	holiday	L11
节奏	jiézòu	n	rhythm	L9
姐姐	jiějie	n	older sister	L2
介绍	jièshào	v/n	to introduce; introduction	L1
今年	jīnnián	n	this year	L1
今天	jīntiān	n	today	L14
金矿	jīnkuàng	n	gold mine	L14
近	jìn	adj	near; close	L5
近期	jìnqī	n	recent time	L14
进	jìn	v	to enter	L7
禁止	jìnzhǐ	v	to prohibit	L14
经常	jīngcháng	adv	often	L4

经典	jīngdiǎn	n	classics	L9
经济学	jīngjìxué	n	economics	L3
经久不衰	jīngjiǔbùshuāi	idiom	ever-lasting	L9
就	jiù	adv	just	L4
举办	jǔbàn	v	to hold (an event)	L12
巨大	jùdà	a	great	L14
觉得	juéde	v	feel	L9

K

开	kāi	v	to open; to operate	L2
开车	kāichē	v	to drive	L5
开始	kāishǐ	v	to begin	L8
开心	kāixīn	adj	happy	L4
看	kàn	v	to look	L5
看不见	kànbùjiàn	v	cannot see	L8
看来	kànlái	v	it seems; it looks; it appears	L13
科技	kējì	n	science and technology	L10
可	kě	adv	quite; very	L11
可能	kěnéng	adv	perhaps	L12
可是	kěshì	conj	but	L12
可以	kěyǐ	a/aux	okay; can; may	L5
课	kè	n	school subject; lesson	L3
客气	kèqi	adj	polite	L7
客人	kèrén	n	guest	L8
客厅	kètīng	n	living room	L8
口	kǒu	n/m	mouth; (measure word for number of people)	L2
口福	kǒufú	n	gourmet's luck	L7
苦力	kǔlì	n	hard laborer	L14
块	kuài	n	measure word for 'dollar'	L11
快餐	kuàicān	n	fast food	L13
快点	kuàidiǎn	adv	faster	L4
快乐	kuàilè	a	happy	L11
会计	kuàijì	n	accountant	L2
会计学	kuàijìxué	n	accounting	L3

L

来	lái	v	to come	L1
来自于	láizìyú	v	to come from	L9
浪费	làngfèi	v	to waste	L10
篮球	lánqiú	n	basketball	L3
劳动	láodòng	n/v	labor	L14
劳工	láogōng	n	laborer	L14
老板	lǎobǎn	n	boss	L2
老师	lǎoshī	n	teacher	L2
了	le	part	(to indicate change of situation)	L2

离	lí	prep	away from	L5
离开	líkāi	v	to leave	L8
亮	liàng	a	bright	L12
里边	lǐbian	n	inside	L3
理发店	lǐfàdiàn	n	barber shop	L5
礼堂	lǐtáng	n	auditorium	L3
礼物	lǐwù	n	gift	L8
历史	lìshǐxué	n	history	L3
两	liǎng	nu	two (used before measure word)	L7
聊天	liáotiān	v	to chat	L4
邻居	línjū	n	neighbor	L5
留	liú	v	to stay; to keep (a guest)	L8
流行	liúxíng	adj/v	popular; to be in vogue	L9
楼房	lóufáng	n	building	L3
路	lù	n	road; way	L5
绿	lǜ	adj	green	L3

M

吗	ma	part	(to form a yes/no question)	L1
妈妈	māma	n	mom	L2
买	mǎi	v	to buy	L5
买单	mǎidān	v	to pay the bill	L
蛮	mán	adv	(collq) quite; rather	L5
满	mǎn	adj	full	L5
满月	mǎnyuè	n	full moon	L12
慢用	mànyòng	idiom	bon appetite	L7
忙	máng	adj	busy	L4
马上	mǎshàng	adv	right away	L8
帽子	màozǐ	n	hat	L10
美	měi	a	beautiful	L3
美籍华人	měijíhuárén	n	Chinese American	L13
美满	měimǎn	a	perfect	L12
美式	měishì	a	American style	L13
每逢佳节倍思亲	měiféngjiājiébèisīqīn	idiom	one is especially homesick on holidays	L12
每	měi	a	every	L4
天	tiān	n	day	L4
没(有)	méi(yǒu)	adv	not (have)	L4
没意思	méiyìsi	a	boring	L12
妹妹	mèimèi	n	younger sister	L2
门	mén	m	(measure word for school subjects)	L3
门口	ménkǒun	door		L8
们	men	pron	(plural suffix for personal pronouns)	L2
面孔	miànkǒng	n	face; looks	L13
面临	miànlín	v	to face	L13
名字	míngzi	n	name (full name or given name)	L1

N

拿手菜	náshǒucài	n	special dish	L7
哪	nǎ	pron	which	L6
哪里	nǎli	pron/idiom	where; (polite response to compliment)	L2
那	nà	pron/conj	that; in that case	L3
那天	nàtiān	pron	the other day; that day	L13
奶	nǎi	n	milk	L7
奶奶	nǎinai	n	grandma (on the father's side)	L2
男	nán	a	male	L14
难道	nándào	adv	isn't it true	L12
难怪	nánguài	idiom	no wonder	L2
呢	ne	part	how about	L1
内地	nèidì	n	inland	L14
能	néng	aux	can; to be able to	L1
你	nǐ	pron	you	L1
你好	nǐhǎo	idiom	hello	L1
年货	niánhuòn	n	goods for new year	L11
年级	niánjí	n	grade; year in school	L1
年轻人	niánqīngrén	n	young people; youths	L10
念	niàn	v	to attend school; to study; to read aloud	L2
您	nín	pron	you (honorific)	L8
牛仔裤	niúzǎikù	n	jeans	L10
农历	nónglì	n/a	lunar calendar; lunar	L11

O

哦	ò	int	oh	L4
偶尔	ǒuěr	adv	occasionally	L1

P

排队	páiduì	v	to stand in line; to queue up	L7
陪	péi	v	to accompany; to keep someone's company	L10
碰到	pèngdào	v	to run into	L10
朋友	péngyǒu	n	friend	L4
皮肤	pífū	n	skin	L13
品尝	pǐncháng	v	to taste; to savor	L7
品种	pǐnzhǒng	n	variety	L7
平时	píngshí	adv	usually	L13

Q

期间	qījiān	n	period	L14
歧视	qíshì	n	discrimination	L14
其他	qítā	adj	other	L6
前	qián	a	former; prior	L11
巧	qiǎo	a	coincidental	L10

亲戚	qīnqi	n	relative	L11
请	qǐng	v	to invite; to request; please	L4
请客	qǐngkè	v	to treat someone to dinner, etc.	L7
轻松活泼	qīngsōnghuópō	adj	light and spirited	L9
祈求	qíqiú	v	to pray for	L12
庆祝	qìngzhù	v	to celebrate	L12
球场	qiúchǎng	n	ball court	L3
区	qū	n	district; borough	L5
取得	qǔdé	v	to achieve	L14
去	qù	v	to go	L3
全	quán	a	all of; complete	L5
劝	quàn	v	to urge	L8
裙子	qúnzi	n	skirt; dress	L10

R

然后	ránhòu	adv	afterward; then	L12
让	ràng	v	to let	L7
热闹	rènao	adj	bustling with noise and excitement	L6
人	rén	n	person; people	L2
人们	rénmen	n	people	L11
认识	rènshi	v	to know; to make someone's acquaintance	L1
容易	róngyì	adj	easy	L9
如	rú	prep	such as; for example	L8
入座	rùzuò	v	take a seat	L8

S

三点一线	sāndiǎnyíxiàn		the same routine	L4
商	shāng	n	business	L1
商场	shāngchǎng	n	mall; shopping center	L10
商店	shāngdiàn	n	shop, store	L3
商人	shāngrén	n	business person	L14
商业	shāngyè	n	business; commerce	L2
赏月	shǎngyuè	v	to enjoy moonlight	L12
上	shàng	prep	on	L6
上班	shàngbān	v	to go to work	L6
上街	shàngjiē	v	to go shopping	L5
上课	shàngkè	v	to go to class	L4
上网	shàngwǎng	v	to go on the internet	L10
上午	shàngwǔ	n	morning	L7
少不了	shǎobuliǎo	v	cannot do without	L12
社团	shètuán	n	club; association	L4
社区	shèqū	n	community	L5
身份	shēnfèn	n	identity	L13
什么	shénme	pron	what	L2
什么时候	shénmeshíhou	adv	some time; one of these days	L3

生活	shēnghuó	n/v	life; to live	L3
生物学	shēngwùxué	n	biology	L3
生意	shēngyì	n	business	L7
省钱	shěngqián	v	to save money	L11
剩下	shèngxià	v	leftover	L11
时候	shíhou	n	time, when	L3
时间	shíjiān	n	time	L5
时尚	shíshàng	n	fashion; fad	L10
时装	shízhuāng	n	fashionable clothing	L10
十分	shífēn	adv	rather; quite	L11
十九	shíjiǔ	nu	nineteen	L1
是	shì	v	to be	L1
世纪	shìjì	n	century	L14
世界	shìjiè	n	world	L9
适可而止	shìkě'érzhǐ	idiom	to know when to stop	L10
市郊	shìjiāo	n	suburb	L5
市区	shìqū	n	city proper	L5
市中心	shìzhōngxīn	n	city center; downtown	L6
收到	shōudào	v	to receive	L11
收拾	shōushi	v	to clean up	L8
首	shǒu	m	(measure word for music)	L9
首饰	shǒushì	n	jewelry; accessory	L10
守夜	shǒuyè	v	to stay up all night	L11
受到	shòudào	v	to be subjected to; to endure	L14
属	shǔ	v	to belong; to be born in the lunar year of	L1
数学	shùxué	n	math	L3
双重	shuāngchóng	a	double	L13
说	shuō	v	to speak	L2
水果	shuǐguǒ	n	fruit	L8
睡觉	shuìjiào	v	to sleep	L10
送	sòng	v	to send, to see someone off	L8
俗话	súhuà	n	saying	L12
虽然	suīrán	conj	although	L5
随着	suízhe	prep	along with	L10
岁	suì	n	years of age	L1
宿舍	sùshè	n	dorm	L4
所以	suóyǐ	conj	so	L12
所有	suóyǒu	adj	all	L7

T

她	tā	pron	she; her	L1
太	tàI	adv	too; extremely	L4
太好了	tàihǎole	idiom	great; wonderful	L4
弹	tán	v	to play (musical instrument); to pluck	L3

套	tào	m	measure word for 'clothes', 'apartment', 'set'	L11
讨论	tǎolùn	v/n	to discuss; discussion	L13
特别	tèbié	adv/adj	especially; special	L4
特产	tèchǎn	n	special product	L8
特点	tèdiǎn	n	characteristics	L9
体力	tǐlì	a/n	physical; physical strength	L14
体育馆	tǐyùguǎn	n	gymnasium	L3
甜	tián	a	sweet	L12
条	tiáo	m	measure word for' street' , 'road', 'river', 'pants', etc. L6
铁路	tiělù	n	railroad	L14
听	tīng	v	to listen	L9
听众	tīngzhòng	n	audience	L9
停车	tíngchē	v/n	to stop a car; to park; parking	L5
停车场	tíngchēchǎng	n	parking lot; parking garage	L5
跳舞	tiàowǔ	v	to dance, dance	L12
通俗	tōngsú	adj	popular	L9
通俗易懂	tōngsúyìdǒng	adj	easy to understand	L9
同学	tóngxué	n	classmate, schoolmate	L13
头发	tóufà	n	hair	L13
头款	tóukuǎn	n	first installment	L11
图书馆	túshūguǎn	n	library	L3
退休	tuìxiū	v	to retire	L2
团圆饭	tuányuánfàn	n	family reunion dinner	L11
脱鞋	tuōxié	v	take off shoes	L8
拖鞋	tuōxié	n	slippers, sandals	L8

W

哇	wa	int	wow	L7
外出	wàichū	v	to travel outside	L11
玩	wán	v	to play; to have fun	L3
完	wán	v	to finish	L8
晚	wǎn	adj/n	late; evening	L6
晚辈	wǎnbèi	n	younger people; junior	L8
晚会	wǎnhuì	n	party	L12
晚上	wǎnshàng	n	evening; night	L12
碗筷	wǎnkuài	n	bowls and chopsticks; empty dishes	L8
万事如意	wànshìrúyì	idiom	everything goes your way	L11
网上	wǎngshàng	a/prep	online; on the internet	L10
忘	wàng	v	to forget	L4
围巾	wéijīn	n	scarf	L10
位	wèi	n/m	seat; (measure word for people)	L7
为	wèi	prep	for	L8
为什么	wèishénme	pron	why	L3
问	wèn	v	to ask	L7

问题	wèntí	n	question; problem	L6
文学	wénxué	n	literature	L3
我	wǒ	pron	I, me	L1
卧室	wòshì	n	bedroom	L8
五花八门	wǔhuābāmén	idiom	multifarious; of a wide variety	L7
舞狮	wǔshī	n	lion dance	L11

X

习惯	xíguàn	v/n	to get used to; habit	L8
喜欢	xǐhuan	v	to like	L3
洗手间	xíshǒujiān	n	bathroom	L8
洗衣店	xǐyīdiàn	n	Laundromat	L5
下车	xiàchē	v	to get off	L6
下次	xiàcì	adv	next time	L7
先	xiān	adv	first	L8
现代	xiàndài	a	modern; contemporary	L9
现在	xiànzài	adv	now	L8
想	xiǎng	v	to want; to think	L3
像	xiàng	prep	like; such as	L9
小	xiǎo	adj	small	L8
小菜	xiǎocài	n	pickles	L7
小炒	xiǎochǎo	n	small stir-fried dish	L7
小时	xiǎoshí	n	hour	L5
小学	xiǎoxué	n	primary school	L2
校园	xiàoyuán	n	campus	L3
谢谢	xièxiè	idiom	thanks	L7
心想事成	xīnxiǎngshìchéng	idiom	all your wishes come true	L11
新	xīn	a	new	L4
新款	xīnkuǎna	n	new style; latest model	L10
新年	xīnnián	n	new year	L11
信息	xìnxī	n	information	L10
兴隆	xīnglóng	adj	brisk (business); prosperous	L7
星期	xīngqī	n	week	L7
星期天	xīngqītiān	n	Sunday	L7
姓	xìng	n/v	family name; to be surnamed	L1
兴趣	xìngqù	n	interest	L13
幸福	xìngfú	a	happy; blessed	L12
修	xiū	v	to build, to fix	L14
修改	xiūgǎi	v/n	to revise; amendment	L14
许多	xǔduō	a	many; a lot of	L12
学	xué	v/n	to study; to learn	L1
学期	xuéqī	n	semester	L3
学生	xuésheng	n	student	L1
学习	xuéxí	v/n	to study; study	L14
学校	xuéxiào	n	school	L3

| 选 | xuǎn | v | to select | L3 |
| 寻找 | xúnzhǎo | v | to seek; to search | L10 |

Y

呀	ya	part	(to soften forcefulness of speech)	L1
压岁钱	yāsuìqián	n	lucky money	L11
研究生	yánjiūshēng	n	graduate student	L2
演唱	yǎnchàng	v	to sing; to perform	L9
演唱会	yǎnchànghuì	n	concert	L9
眼睛	yǎnjing	n	eye	L13
羊	yáng	n	ram	L1
要	yào	v/aux	to want; to need; to be going to	L2
爷爷	yéye	n	grandpa (on the father's side)	L2
也	yě	adv	also	L1
夜	yè	n	eve; night	L10
医	yī	n	medical science	L2
医生	yīshēng	n	doctor	L14
医院	yīyuàn	n	hospital	L5
衣服	yīfu	n	clothes;shirt or blouse	L10
移民	yímín	v/n	to immigrate; immigrant	L2
移民法	yímínfǎ	n	immigration law	L14
英文	yīngwén	n	English language	L13
以后	yǐhòu	prep	after	L8
已经	yǐjīng	adv	already	L2
一点	yìdiǎn	adj	a little	L8
一点也不	yìdiǎnyěbù	idiom	not at all	L4
一般	yìbān	adv	generally	L5
一定	yídìng	adv	certainly; definitely	L4
一边	yìbiān	adv	at the same time	L7
一共	yīgòng	adv	altogether	L11
一起	yìqǐ	adv	together	L1
一下	yíxià	adv	a little while	L1
(一)些	(yì)xiē	a/adv	some; unspecified number	L3
一言为定	yìyánwéidìng	idiom	it's a deal	L3
一阵子	yízhènzi	adv	a while	L12
(一)直	(yì)zhí	adv	all the time	L10
意思	yìsi	n	meaning	L10
因此	yīncǐ	conj	therefore	L13
因为	yīnwèi	conj	because	L3
音乐	yīnyuè	n	music	L3
银行	yínháng	n	bank	L11
应该	yīnggāi	aux	should	L8
应有尽有	yīngyǒujìnyǒu	idiom	all encompassing	L9
影响	yǐngxiǎng	v/n	to influence; influence	L9
涌入	yǒngrù	v/n	to pour in; influx	L14

由	yóu	prep	by (somebody); from (some place or something)	L9
友好	yǒuhǎo	adj	friendly	L5
游戏	yóuxì	n	games	L3
游泳池	yóuyǒngchí	n	swimming pool	L3
有	yǒu	v	to have	L2
有趣	yǒuqù	a	interesting	L12
有时	yǒushí	adv	sometimes	L4
有意思	yǒuyìsi	adj	interesting	L4
又	yòu	adv	again (in the past)	L2
与	yǔ	prep	with; and	L10
愉快	yúkuài	a	happy	L12
娱乐	yúlè	n/a	leisure; past-time; fashionable	L10
远	yuǎn	adj	far	L5
院子	yuànzi	n	yard	L12
月	yuè	n	moon; month	L12
月饼	yuèbing	n	moon cake	L12
月亮	yuèliang	n	moon	L12
越来越	yuèláiyuè	adv	more and more	L10
浴室	yùshì	n	bathroom	L12

Z

早	zǎo	adj/n	early; morning	L6
早茶	zǎochá	n	morning tea	L7
早点	zǎodiǎn	adv	earlier	L3
早年	zǎonián	adv	long ago	L2
早期	zǎoqī	a	early	L14
在	zài	prep/part	at (a place); (progressive particle)	L2
怎么	zěnme	adv	how; how come	L8
站	zhàn	n/v	stop; to stand	L5
张灯结彩	zhāngdēngjiécǎi	idiom	to decorate with lanterns and paper cuts	L11
长	zhǎng	v	to grow	L13
长大	zhǎngdà	v	to grow up	L13
长辈	zhǎngbèi	n	older people; senior	L8
招待	zhāodài	v	to treat; to entertain	L8
着	zhe	part	(to indicate continuous or stationary status)	L6
这	zhè	pron	this	L1
这么	zhème	adv	so, such	L2
这些	zhèxiē	pron	these	L13
真	zhēn	adv	really	L7
政府	zhèngfǔ	n	government	L14
正好	zhènghǎo	adv	happen to; exactly	L4
知道	zhīdào	v	to know	L14
直到	zhídào	conj	until	L8
只	zhǐ	adv	only	L3
之母	zhīmǔ	n	(arch.) mother of	L9

之一	zhīyī	pron	one of	L12
钟	zhōng	n	clock; o'clock	L10
中国话	zhōngguóhuà	n	spoken Chinese	L13
中秋节	zhōngqiūjié	n	Mid-Autumn Festival	L12
中心	zhōngxīn	n	center	L3
中学	zhōngxué	n	secondary school	L2
中文	zhōngwén	n	Chinese language	L1
重要	zhòngyào	adj	important	L9
周末	zhōumò	n	weekend	L5
自己	zìjǐ	pron	self	L1
自我	zìwǒ	a	self	L1
主人	zhǔrèn	n	host	L8
主修	zhǔxiū	v	to major in	L1
主要	zhǔyào	adj/adv	main; mainly	L6
住	zhù	v	to reside; to live	L2
祝	zhù	v	to wish	L11
注意	zhùyì	v	to pay attention	L10
专业	zhuānyè	n	major	L1
准备	zhǔnbèi	v	to prepare	L8
桌子	zhuōzi	n	table	L7
自习	zìxí	v	to study by oneself	L4
总是	zǒngshì	adv	always	L5
走	zǒu	n	to walk	L4
走路	zǒulù	v	to walk	L5
最	zuì	adv	most	L6
座	zuò	m	(measure word for town or building)	L3
做	zuò	v	to do	L2
做客	zuòkè	v	to be a guest	L5
坐	zuò	v	to sit	L5
坐车	zuòchē	v	to ride in a car, bus, or subway	L5
作品	zuòpǐn	n	composition	L9

CPSIA information can be obtained
at www.ICGtesting.com
Printed in the USA
LVHW051515151222
735238LV00008B/525

9 781721 976669